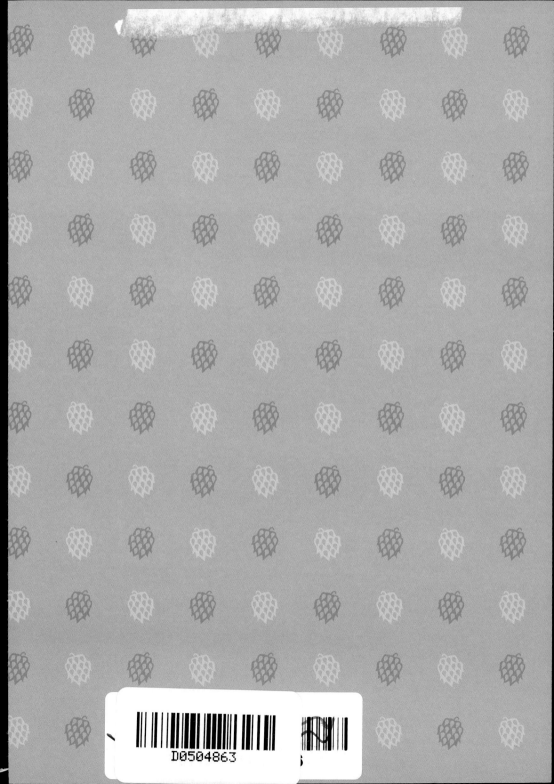

WISDOM *for* HOME BREWERS

WISDOM *for* HOME BREWERS

500 TIPS & RECIPES
FOR MAKING GREAT BEER

TED BRUNING & NIGEL SADLER

First published in the UK in 2014 by

Apple Press

74-77 White Lion Street

London N1 9PF

www.apple-press.com

ISBN: 978-1-84543-575-2

Conceived, designed, and produced by

Quid Publishing

Level 4 Sheridan House

114 Western Road

Hove BN3 1DD

www.quidpublishing.com

Every effort has been made to ensure that all of the information in this book
is correct at the time of publication. This book is not intended to replace
manufacturers' instructions in the use of their products – always follow their
safety guidelines. The author, publisher and copyright holder assume no
responsibility for any injury, loss or damage caused or sustained as a
consequence of the use and application of the contents of this book.

Printed in China by 1010 Printing International Ltd.

10 9 8 7 6 5 4 3 2 1

Dedicated to the memory of Dave Line (1942–80), the pioneer and still the guru.

CONTENTS

INTRODUCTION

People start home brewing for all sorts of reasons. For some it's thrift. For others it's frustration at the limited choice they can find in off-licences and pubs. But for most, perhaps, it's love of the craft: home brewing can be endlessly absorbing. And if it's your personal goal to brew beer as good as anything you can buy – given time, you can!

GETTING STARTED

Like all craft-based hobbies, home brewing takes a lot of time, effort and (potentially!) expense, although some would argue that the reward is greater than other crafts. The idea of having a constant stream of delicious – and cheap! – beer on tap obviously appeals, or you wouldn't be reading this. But before you plunge in and make the commitment, ask yourself a few searching questions.

BASIC TRAINING

TIP 1: *Ask yourself how much you really love beer*

⚙ Your ambition as a brewer is going to be largely determined by how much you really love beer. Much of the satisfaction of any hobby is in the 'doing'; given the time and attention (not to mention money) you're going to dedicate, brewing has to be something you enjoy and are interested in. You wouldn't build your own boat if you were terrified of water! So what, exactly, is your relationship with beer? Is it a subject you find endlessly fascinating? Or is it a commodity you take for granted but wouldn't mind having a go at one day? The answer to that question will dictate what sort of home brewer you're going to be.

TIP 2: *Count how many kinds of beer you've had in the last month*

⚙ Actually, you don't have to do this – or at least not in any great detail, because that would just be weird. The question, really, is whether you always have a glass of the usual when you go out and always reach for the same six-pack of cans in the off-licence, or whether you're the kind of drinker who enjoys new sensations, new flavours, new experiences. If the former, there's no reason why you shouldn't brew perfectly pleasant beer – beer you're quite happy to offer your friends, and beer they're quite happy to be offered – without getting obsessive about it. If the latter, your whole life might be about to change.

TIP 3: *Make a list of all the beer styles you can think of*

● This is a semi-serious exercise designed to help you decide whether your homebrewing equipment is going to end up in the shed or if you're going to get hours of pleasure out of the brewing and litres of pleasure out of the drinking. If you're still in single figures and scratching your head, this may not be the hobby for you. If you've listed 30-odd, stop trying to think of more and focus instead on the differences between them. You'll probably have brewed them all one day. If you've got to more than 50 and you're still going strong, see a doctor.

TIP 4: *Go for a drink!*

● Now it's time to go on a journey of exploration. Go to your local bars, supermarkets, and off-licences, drinking as promiscuously as your local retail trade allows. Not all in one day, of course; but getting to know your beer means drinking not only lots of different styles – lagers, pale ales, stouts, brown ales, wheat beers, you name it – but also competing versions of the same style. This is not an excuse for a protracted bacchanal of beer – you'll be drinking critically and taking notes.

TIP 5: *Take advantage of beer festivals*

Unless you live in a great metropolis with a lively and varied bar scene and one or more specialist beer shops, you're inevitably going to be restricted in the range of beers you can buy. That's where the beer festival comes in – that brief eye in the hurricane of life when you can book a few days off work, invest in a notebook with a wipe-down cover, and get sampling. British beer festivals aren't quite as taster-friendly as American ones because British law sets the minimum draft dispense at a third of a pint, which rather limits the number of beers you can sensibly sample. But anyway, do the best you can, and either take the bus or give your car keys to a teetotal friend. Oh, and remember – take notes! There'll be questions later.

TIP 6: *Drink with your brain*

Tasting beer as seriously as you would taste fine wines seems somehow inappropriate. The price of a bottle of really good wine may be enough to justify all that solemn swirling, sniffing, gargling and spitting, but, hey – beer is just a drink! For the dedicated brewer, though, evaluating beer is a deadly serious business, not only to assess the results of your latest brew but also to make sure that you can brew it consistently again and again. You may have recorded the recipe and the process in minute detail, but the only really reliable record of the result is a trained and accurate brain.

TIP 7: *Ask yourself: What does the Pastoral Symphony smell of? How smooth is red?*

⬤ Describing one sensation in terms of another is impossible. So when tasters record flavours and aromas they have to do it in terms of other flavours and aromas; and to communicate their findings they use a common language of established descriptions. It may be amusing listening to wine experts talking about flint, tobacco, leather, wet dog and so on, but each of these expressions has been agreed as identifying a specific flavour component. Some really top-notch tasters have gone beyond analogous terminology and dive straight into biochemistry, describing what they're tasting in terms of esters, polyphenols and so forth. For most, it's more practical to try to capture a sense-memory of peaches, or cloves, or bubblegum or new-mown grass, and then retrieve them as needed. It can be done. You just have to focus hard on whatever you're eating or drinking or smelling and give it a name. That way you establish a mental filing system that actually works.

TIP 8: *Look before you sip*

⬤ 'You don't drink with your eyes' is the British bar owner's usual protest when he has to pour away a pint of cloudy ale. And many serious professional tasters take this maxim a step further and use blue drinking-glasses so their noses and palates won't be influenced by the evidence of their eyes. But on your voyage of exploration you want to capture as much data as possible, so before deploying your nose, hold your glass up to the light and consider what you see. Not only will the brilliance tell you about the condition of the beer (unless it's an opalescent wheat beer or an impenetrably murky stout), but the colour of the beer will tell you a fair bit about the blend of malts used to make it.

TIP 9: Sniff out the truth

The 7,500 or so taste buds in our mouth and covering our tongues can detect five flavours – sweet, sour, salty, bitter and umami (richness). It's now known that all of the taste buds can detect all of the flavours, rendering obsolete the old-fashioned tongue-map that placed the bitterness receptors at the back and gave beer-tasters their excuse for swallowing rather than spitting. But it's the nose that does the really sensitive work. That's where the separate components are identified; and that's why, before you're allowed to drink, you have to give the glass a good swirl, cupping your hand over it to hold the vapours in, and have an almighty sniff. (It is advisable not to have too full a glass or the swirling can cause embarrassment!)

TIP 10: Can you smell the hops yet?

The first aromas to assail your nostrils should come from the hops. The most popular aroma hop varieties these days seem to be primarily citrusy, but that covers quite a wide spectrum from sharp grapefruit to soft lemon. Or you might get floral notes from European hops such as Saaz and Hallertau. Some more traditional ale varieties such as Fuggle have deeper, earthier scents; or if they're fruity it might be greengage or even marmalade you detect. But there's no right or wrong. The equipment in your nose and brain are personal to you; the important thing is to concentrate on what you're smelling and file it away in your sense memory banks.

TIP 11: *Biscuit, anyone?*

The malt grist also contributes to the aroma of the beer, if perhaps less so (normally) than the hops. Given that the malt is basically cooked flour – twice-cooked, in fact – then it's no surprise that the aroma that most people associate with malt is commonly described as 'biscuity'. But some malts, especially carapils and crystal malt, also yield wonderfully rich vine fruit, toffee and caramel scents. If that doesn't make you want to rush off and brew a lovely copper-coloured beer with a soupçon of crystal malt and an all-Fuggle hop regime, then there's something wrong with you!

TIP 12: *Okay – now drink!*

You may now take a swig of beer. Not a sip, a swig. Fill your mouth. Don't swallow yet. Hold the beer for a while, roll it around your tongue, and concentrate. Some tasters even do that funny slurpy thing that wine-tasters do, but it's not an easy art to master! The point of it is to allow the vapours to rise off the beer and seep into your nasal cavity, because you're not only tasting it with your tongue, you're having a second go at smelling it as well. Holding the beer in your mouth for a while also gives you time to isolate and classify each separate flavour component – a skill acquired only through practice, you'll be pleased to hear.

TIP 13: Identify off-flavours

Well, things can and do go wrong, and most people are unlikely to find out about them until they've taken a mouthful (experienced tasters can detect them by nose alone, but more often your first shot of off-flavours will come as you're tasting the beer). It won't happen to you often in pubs or at festivals because few brewers would let their product leave the brewery with any taint. But imperfections arising from poor fermentation or incorrect temperatures at various stages can generate all kinds of off-flavours such as sweetcorn (dimethyl sulphide), green apples (acetaldehyde), harshness (higher alcohols), butterscotch (diacetyl), astringency (mouth puckering, due to tannin) and vinegar (sour/sharp, due to bacterial infection). Log these just as assiduously as you log the nicer flavours: once you've started brewing, this item in your library of sense memories will become the sonic screwdriver in your troubleshooting toolkit.

TIP 14: Visit breweries

The final stage in your education is to visit breweries and see people actually doing what you plan to do yourself. And don't take 'visiting breweries' to mean going as a tourist to nice well-laid out brewery museums and visitors' centres with guided tours and a free session in the sample room afterward. Although fun (and there's no reason why you shouldn't enjoy such an excursion), it's much better to make friends with a local microbrewer – buying a 17L (4-gallon) polypin of ale for a party is a good way of introducing yourself – and get the full one-to-one conducted tour. You might even ingratiate yourself further by volunteering for some of the more arduous or boring tasks that few full-time brewers even pretend to enjoy – cask-washing, say, or bottling, or even digging out the mash tun. Once you've shovelled out a couple of hundred kilograms of soggy malt, you'll either run a mile – or you'll be hooked for life!

FIRST STEPS

TIP 15: *Think before you shop*

🌑 Home brewing is one of those hobbies, like golf and fishing, that can cost you a small fortune – or even a large one – if you don't approach it with forethought and caution. You can easily march into a homebrew shop or visit a homebrew website and spend hundreds of dollars on the latest gleaming gadgetry, which might be useful to you much later on but will probably end up in the shed if you splash out on it today. So for the moment at least, put away your plastic – you may even already possess much of the equipment you need!

TIP 16: *Make time*

🌑 Brewing takes time and patience. A typical brew day can last 8 hours, and even though you might spend quite a bit of it sitting around waiting, you need to make sure you've allowed yourself time to finish what you've started without having to rush, because rushing will, as we all know, lead to silly mistakes! So send everybody else to the movies, the park, the beach, or whatever, and then lock yourself away in the kitchen.

TIP 17: *Organise your spaces*

⚙ If home brewing is a branch of cookery, then the home brewer's natural habitat must be the kitchen. It has everything you need: power sockets, running water, wipedown surfaces, a floor you can mop (home brewing can be messy) and, crucially, different levels. But not everything's going to happen in the kitchen. Fermentation will take a week or so at a constant temperature of 18–22°C (64–72°F) (low- to mid-strength ales) or 2–3 months at 1–2°C (34–36°F) (lager). You need to work out in advance where in the home you can reserve the appropriate spaces – classically, the cupboard under the stairs and the garage. And then you'll need yet another space to stow your equipment when not in use. Earmark spaces that are out of everybody's way, and where your equipment, whether working or in store, won't be tripped over all the time.

TIP 18: *Buy a good strong step stool*

⚙ Typically, you'll be brewing in 25L (6½-gallon) batches. Several times during the brewing process, 25L of hot liquid will have to be poured from a vessel on your work surface to a receiving vessel below, and the receiving vessel will in turn have to be hoisted up onto the work surface. Standing the receiving vessel on a good solid step stool has two advantages. First, anything standing on the floor is at risk from pet dogs, small children or clumsy adults. Secondly, standing the vessel on a stool reduces both the angle you'll have to bend to pick it up, which will save your back a fair bit of strain (25L = 25kg, 55lb), and the distance the hot liquid will have to fall, which means less spatter – and you don't want your kitchen spattered with hot sticky wort! So, although a good strong step stool might be an odd starting-point for equipping your home brewery, it's an essential piece of gear.

TIP 19: *Keep it clean*

⬤ There's a lot of sugar involved in brewing. In fact, the first step in the process, mashing, is simply the conversion of malt starch into fermentable malt sugar (or maltose). All kinds of bugs and bacteria just love sugar and will ruin your brew if allowed to feast on it, so all surfaces need to be clean at all times. Chapter 8, Troubleshooting, sets out details of your two-step cleaning and sanitising regime. Household stain removers, detergents or even bleach are fine for cleaning used equipment, but for the second step – sanitising before use – brewers generally prefer sodium metabisulphite. It works by producing lethal sulphur dioxide gas (SO_2) and doesn't need rinsing off, making it especially suitable for sterilising or sanitising the interiors of vessels, pipes, bottles, etc. But for sanitising work surfaces and the exteriors of vessels, a very weak solution of household bleach (1–1.5% will do) is perfectly adequate. A proprietary solution such as Milton fluid is dilute enough to disinfect babies' bottles perfectly safely. Keep it handy – in the form of spray or, more convenient still, wipes – and wipe down everything within reach, especially after you've touched it. Make this an inflexible habit.

Campden tablets

TIP 20: Start with an extract-based kit

A brewing kit is simplicity itself. It comprises a can of ready-hopped malt extract and a sachet of yeast. The extract is diluted with hot water as instructed and then allowed to cool, before being pitched with the yeast and then left to ferment. Among the first pieces of equipment you'll need are a 25L (6½-gallon) brewing bucket and a good thermometer (see the next tip). Originally, kits like this were generic – 'mild', 'bitter', 'stout', 'lager' and so forth – but then someone had the bright idea of making branded kits that would in theory replicate one of your favourite beers. Of course, they can never be exactly the same because the version you buy at the bar hasn't first been concentrated by evaporation and then reconstituted with tap water. But, made carefully, they can be pretty close.

TIP 21: Get a decent thermometer

You really do need a good thermometer because there are stages in the brewing process where temperature is critical, even if you're still at the kit stage. In fact, nothing is likelier to ruin a kit than poor temperature control (other than poor hygiene, that is). The bathroom thermometer simply isn't accurate or robust enough for use in home brewing, so get a good one from your homebrew supplier – either an old-style glass one (get several – glass breaks!) or an electronic one (safer!). And use it properly and carefully; for example, observe the correct immersion depth or you'll get inaccurate and inconsistent readings.

TIP 22: A hydrometer is essential

⬤ You absolutely need a hydrometer. It's going to be your best friend. It's a simple enough device – no more than a calibrated glass float in a test tube or trial jar – but it will tell you what your beer is doing during fermentation by monitoring its gravity. During fermentation the gravity (the measure of a beer's density) will fall, and the hydrometer will sink, as the sugars are consumed. This will give you an idea of its strength and will tell you when fermentation is complete. But your hydrometer doesn't only measure the approximate strength of your beer; it also acts as a health check. If the gravity stops falling you may have a stuck ferment (see page 189) and will need to take action.

TIP 23: Choose either type of hydrometer

⬤ Just to confuse you, there are two types of hydrometer. One will measure the density of wort at 15.6°C (60°F), the other at 20°C (68°F). It doesn't really matter which type you choose, but get the biggest you can because it will be easier to read, and buy two or three. They're made of very thin glass and they're cylindrical, which means they can roll off surfaces and shatter.

TIP 24: Test away from the brew where possible

⬤ As with a glass thermometer, bear in mind that a broken hydrometer means broken glass, which is obviously something of a hazard! To minimise the risk of you or your friends and relations cutting the insides of your mouths to ribbons, do your gravity testing well away from your brewing kit.

TIP 25: *Get a refractometer*

● Quicker than a hydrometer, a refractometer is a simple handheld device that will set you back a few quid but is dead easy to use. It relies on the principle of light bending (refraction). You put a drop of wort on a glass prism, close the lid, hold the whole contraption up to a light source and look through the eyepiece to see where the coloured line is on the grid. Most are calibrated in units called 'Brix', so for a rough rule of thumb multiply the reading by four to give degrees gravity. There are even flashy electronic ones out there if money is no object!

TIP 26: *Buy a boiler...*

● So far your brewery consists of one 25L (6½-gallon) bucket (with lid and stout handles), one or more heavy-duty thermometers, ditto hydrometers and a few things you've borrowed from the kitchen, such as a measuring pitcher and a long-handled wooden spoon (the longer the handle the better). Brewing kits generally don't need boiling, but unhopped malt extract mashes do, so your first major investment (after the thermometer) will be an insulated electric boiler of 30–50L (8–13 gallons), preferably with an integral false bottom of fine wire mesh to strain the spent hops (although you can buy this separately).

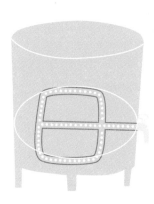

TIP 27: ... Or a brewpot

⚙ An easier solution might be to invest in a good-quality brewpot: a stainless steel or aluminium vessel ranging from a straightforward catering-size stockpot that stands on the hob to a highly specialised version with its own integral thermometer and gas jets. The stockpot is the cheaper option, although it probably takes more energy to bring it up to the boil. Its greatest drawback, though, is that it has no tap. If you want to avoid messing around with pitchers or siphons, or having to manoeuvre a heavy metal vessel full of hot sticky liquid, buy a purpose-made brewpot with an outlet valve! (A good stockpot will still be useful, though.)

TIP 28: Buy a self-heating boiler

⚙ In Britain, with its higher mains voltage, a boiler with its own heating element is not only feasible but mandatory. You could use a perfectly ordinary catering boiler or tea-urn, such as a Burco, with a wire-mesh false bottom bought separately; but as you'll be making repeated use of your homebrew supplies shop you might as well get a boiler there. The most basic models aren't all that expensive, and a thermostatic one will also double for purposes such as descaling your tap water and getting your sparging water up to the correct heat.

TIP 29: *Alternatively, make your own boiler*

It is possible to construct a perfectly good boiler of your own for a fraction of the price. Basically, it's another big bucket (at least 30L [8 gallons], preferably 50L [13 gallons]) with a lid, one hole at the bottom for the tap and either two more holes for a brace of kettle elements or one for an immersion heater element. Separate kettle elements are harder to come by these days, and immersion heater elements have the advantage of being controlled via a thermostat – not that your boiler needs a thermostat. When you're hopping your wort you want it boiling. But if it does have a thermostat it will double as a hot-liquor tank, since when mashing and sparging liquor the temperature shouldn't be anywhere near boiling.

TIP 30: *Next thing you'll want is a fermenting vessel*

Or, to put it more bluntly, an oversized polypropylene bucket with a stout handle, a lid and a tap. It should be oversized because your beer will – or should – throw a deep, rocky head in the early stages of fermentation, which you should keep inside the vessel, not all over the kitchen. The beer might stay in the fermentation vessel (FV) for a week or thereabouts, so if you haven't been able to find anywhere with a pretty constant temperature you will want either to improvise an insulating jacket – got any old duvets in a neglected bottom drawer? – or splash out on an insulated vessel. The basic FV is another of those items that will – even when you have graduated to an Italian-made stainless steel cylindro-conical with floating lid – prove its worth in all sorts of subsidiary roles.

TIP 31: *Your FV needn't be a bucket*

◉ Many home brewers prefer to ferment their beer in a carboy – a 30L (8-gallon) glass or even plastic bottle – rather than a bucket. (If plastic, check the recycling code on the bottom; anything less than #1 may be gas-porous and could let oxygen in and CO_2 out.) The carboy has two main advantages over the bucket: the surface area of the liquid is much smaller, reducing the risk of airborne infection, and it is transparent, allowing you to see what's going on inside. Particularly useful against yeast flocculation.

TIP 32: *Remember that carboys have their drawbacks too*

◉ The obvious one is that they're harder to clean. But not much harder. The narrow mouth makes brushing a tricky business, even with a specially designed right-angled brush, but a really effective solvent such as a stain remover should do most of the brush's work just as well. The bigger drawback is that they're harder to access when in use: if you need to rouse or aerate your secondary fermentation you have little option but to pick the whole thing up and swirl it bodily as if at a barn dance.

TIP 33: *Fill your carboy with a funnel, empty it with a siphon*

◉ The narrow mouth presents a few more challenges, especially in filling and emptying. The best way to fill a carboy for primary fermentation is with a huge funnel, which will allow you to hold the outlet hose from your boiler or wort chiller as high up as possible to get as much air as you can into the wort without covering the kitchen in sticky splashes. You will need a siphon to transfer your beer from the FV to the conditioning tank (see Tip 34, page 28) for its second (anaerobic) fermentation, and then from conditioning tank to bottling bucket because carboys don't have taps. Make sure your siphon is fitted with a sediment trap on the end that sits inside the carboy.

TIP 34: *Use an autosiphon*

⬤ Home winemakers just stick the end of the siphon tube in their mouths and suck. This is okay for them because the higher alcohol content of wine reduces the risk of infection and because, typically, they're only dealing with 5L (1¼ gallons) at a time. Brewers, though, should use an autosiphon, a cheap and ingenious vacuum pump that works like a bicycle pump, except that, instead of blowing, it sucks.

TIP 35: *Keep the bugs at bay*

⬤ A carboy, just like the winemaker's demijohn, needs an airlock of some kind to keep airborne pathogens out. For the secondary fermentation an ordinary bubble trap will do the job perfectly; but the primary fermentation might require different equipment because of the big foamy head that can and indeed should be thrown up. If you're fermenting a 25L (6½-gallon) brew in a 30L (8-gallon) carboy it's unlikely to throw enough of a head to surge out through the airlock, but it does happen. Use a blow tube instead. This is an ordinary but quite long siphon tube with one end stuck through the hole in the carboy's bung and the other (weighted) end submerged in 500ml (1 pint) or so of sanitiser in a big bowl or small bucket. This functions in exactly the same way as an airlock but if the head does force its way out, it'll all be contained in the bowl/bucket.

TIP 36: *Create a 'musical' airlock for the secondary fermentation*

⬤ Buy a whoopee cushion and cut off its neck. Sanitise it well and roll it firmly onto the mouth of your carboy, securing it with a rubber band or a cable tie if necessary. Essentially, what you have is a self-sealing one-way valve that will let CO_2 out but nothing in, exactly like the respirator tube on an old-fashioned gas mask. And every time it vents, it will announce that it is doing so with a sound that you will recognise. If you no longer hear its announcements, you will know that the fermentation has stopped. A bit flippant, perhaps, but a good way of alerting you to a stuck ferment! (For more on airlocks, see Tip 72, page 46.)

TIP 37: *Procure a barrel*

⬤ Once your primary fermentation is over, the beer will want a week or two's secondary fermentation or conditioning before it's ready to drink, so you'll need another insulated vessel (with tap and sturdy handles, of course) ready for the purpose. The perfect thing for the job is the standard 25L (8-gallon) polycask universally used by craft cidermakers in Britain for draft dispense. The only adaptation required for brewing purposes is that the screw top needs a built-in pressure valve, or else the whole thing will explode. Fortunately, this is a standard item of a homebrew supplier's stock. More sophisticated (and expensive) pressure barrels are available, but this will do for now.

TIP 38: Experience the joy of extract

● The next step up from using kits is brewing with malt extract. This is simply sweet wort (ie, beer before hopping and fermentation) condensed either by evaporation or vacuum into a thick, sweet, treacly sludge. All you have to do is rehydrate it, boil it with hops and ferment the result. The condensation process naturally affects the flavour of the malt, but not too dramatically; the two upsides for the novice home brewer are that using extracts simplifies the whole process and cuts out the variables/errors/cock-ups that can and do arise in full-mash brewing. In fact, some home brewers never progress to full-mash brewing and get perfectly palatable results from extract. All the recipes given in Chapter 10 can be made using malt extract; if there are any specialist grains in the recipe, steep them in warm water at 65°C (149°F) and add the resultant liquid to the dissolved extract.

TIP 39: Use your liquid malt extract fresh!

● Left too long in the can, liquid malt extract (LME) can develop an off-flavour known as 'tang'. It's essential, therefore, to check the expiration date on the can before you part with your pennies. And if you find you're stuck with a part-used can, you're probably better off using the leftovers to bake with rather than letting it go stale in the refrigerator. Or just spread it on toast! Liquid malt extract is also quite difficult to work with – it'll make an unholy mess of your kitchen scales, for instance, but you can always measure it instead of weighing it: a kilogram of malt extract has a volume of 710ml (¾qt). Dissolve liquid malt extract in hot water.

MALT

TIP 40: *Remember that DME keeps longer*

● Malt extract is also sold in a powdered, or more accurately crystalline, form known as DME or spraymalt. Some say that the added level of processing detracts from the flavour, but it is easier to store and handle, being not so bulky and sticky, and it has a much longer shelf life. DME can also be substituted at any stage of the process where sugar is called for – making a yeast starter, for example, or priming bottled beers. It can be used in baking too, and – or so it's said – produces interesting variations of custard and ice cream. DME dissolves better in cold-to-warm water.

TIP 41: *You can convert all grain to LME or DME*

● Base malt conversion is simple. For an equivalent weight of LME, multiply the number of kilograms or pounds of base pale or lager malt by a factor of 0.75. For example, 5kg (11lb) of lager malt equals 3.75kg (8¼lb) of LME. To convert to DME the factor is 0.6, so 5kg of pale malt equates to 3kg (6³⁄₅lb) of dried malt extract.

TIP 42: *Try blending extract with full grain*

● Extract is available these days in almost as many varieties as there are types of malt, from pale ale to black. This means that deciding to stick with extract shouldn't limit the range of beers you can brew. That said, some of the more specialised malts are only available as grain, as are, naturally enough, the flaked and unmalted grains you'll want to play with. But don't worry! You can always make a hybrid mash from a base of extract blended with special grains of various sorts.

EQUIPMENT

Now we come to the fun bit – shopping! There are people for whom any kind of craft or hobby is a glorious excuse to whip out the plastic and buy up every item of shiny hi-tech gear imaginable. Anglers, golfers, cyclists – some of them just can't keep their wallets in their pockets. The good news is that home brewing offers them plenty of opportunity to spend money. The better news is it's not compulsory. Less-flashy equipment works just as well; and if you're the mechanical type, you can improvise to your heart's content.

DO THE MASH – DO THE MONSTER MASH

TIP 43: *As always before shopping, make a list*

🌐 These are the stages in brewing, and you'll need a vessel for each one:

1. **WATER TREATMENT:** boiler or brewpot (which you already have)
2. **MASHING:** mash tun
3. **RUNNING OFF:** wort receiver
4. **BOILING WITH HOPS:** boiler or brewpot
5. **RUNNING OFF:** lauter tun or hop back
   (your mash tun will serve as a hop back)
6. **PRIMARY FERMENTATION:** fermenting vessel (FV)
   and optional holding tank
7. **SECONDARY FERMENTATION:** pressure barrel or carboy with airlock
8. **BOTTLING:** bottling barrel
9. **KEGGING:** two Cornelius kegs and a gas bottle

You will by now have spotted that the roles of wort receiver, optional holding tank and bottling barrel can all be played by the same vessel. As the mash tun, boiler and FV are the Holy Trinity of brewing, I have christened this vessel the Fourth Bucket. There are various gadgets and accessories to buy as well: a chilling coil, siphon tubes, lots of washing machine/dishwasher hose, lengths of metal tubing and a brewing stick, among other things. And having two or three spare brewing buckets as well is always handy!

TIP 44: Step up to full mash – get a mash tun

● To make the leap from malt extract to full mash you need a mash tun. But what is this hallowed object, the mash tun? Well, like most things in home brewing, it's a bucket – one that is well insulated and has sturdy handles, a tight-fitting lid and a tap at the bottom. This is the vessel in which your malt grist will be steeped in hot water to convert the starch granules in the malt endosperm into the simple sugars on which your yeast will feast. Insulation is its most important feature: the mash will have to maintain its temperature for up to an hour and a half without losing more than a degree at most.

TIP 45: Look at the cheapest option first

● The cheapest option is the one you make yourself: a bucket with a hole cut in it for the tap, snugly wrapped up (cover the top too) in foam camping mattresses, an offcut of hot-water cylinder jacket or just an old duvet or sleeping bag. If you do make your own, check its heat-retention properties first by filling it with hot water, taking its temperature, closing it up for 90 minutes and then taking its temperature again. You might have to do this more than once, adding more insulation as required.

TIP 46: Check out the high-tech option

● Umm, there isn't one, really. A mash tun just isn't a high-tech item. The most common alternative to the humble bucket is a picnic or camping cool box with a tap fitted. You don't even have to fit the tap yourself, because homebrew suppliers sell them ready-drilled for next to nothing. The insulation on these can be rather skimpy, and the lids aren't insulated at all, so you'll want to test it as above and have that old quilt handy. Avoid mash tuns with thermostatically controlled heating elements: they can be unreliable and may cook the mash... and you're making beer, not porridge!

TIP 47: Don't forget the filter

⬤ Ah yes. One thing every mash tun needs is a filtration system, so that when you run off the wort at the end of the mash the spent malt remains behind. As the malt has been coarsely ground to produce a kind of flour, the residue is made up of small sticky particles that can literally gum up the works, so the filter has to be fairly fine. If you buy the adapted picnic box you'll find it comes with a slotted tube matrix – a long piece of copper tubing shaped to fit the bottom of the box and scored with slots too small to allow the malt particles through – that attaches to the tap. If you're making your own mash tun you can buy a slotted tube matrix. Alternatively, if you've got a vise and a hacksaw at home, you can make your own.

TIP 48: Fit a false bottom

⬤ Finally, a removable false bottom (slotted finely or drilled with small holes of no bigger than a millimetre) and placed 1.25cm (½in) above the filter/outlet is an added bonus if you can get or make one. This replicates commercial mash tun design and helps keep the weight of the grain bed off the filter. It's especially important if your tube matrix is plastic rather than copper; even braided plastic tubing can easily collapse, and the action of stirring can cause flexible tubing to kink.

TIP 49: Use a grain bag

⬤ A grain bag is a big, fairly fine-mesh bag that goes into the mash tun and folds down over the rim. Three things to watch for, though: the bag should be secured to the rim of the vessel either with a drawstring or bulldog clips; it needs to fit snugly, or you won't be able to sparge; and it needs to sit on a trivet so it doesn't block the outflow. An upside-down bowl will do perfectly, so long as it's deep enough to keep the grain bag clear of the outflow.

TIP 50: *Give the grain a shower*

⚫ Sparging is the process of sprinkling the grain with hot water, usually at around 79°C (174°F), while running the wort out of the mash tun to rinse out the very last of the sugars and to switch off the enzyme activity. It's one of the trickiest arts to master in the whole process, yet it requires perhaps the simplest piece of equipment – nothing more complicated, in fact, than the small watering can you use to water your houseplants with. The only thing to be sure of is that the rose on the end of the watering can's spout has the finest holes you can get.

TIP 51: *A piece of aluminium foil will do the job*

⚫ Another very popular way of sparging makes use of a piece of aluminium foil and a pitcher. You lay a sheet – preferably a double sheet – of evenly perforated foil, cut to fit the mash tun snugly, over the top of the mash and, as the tun drains, you gently drizzle your sparge liquor over the foil. It's a delicate job. You need to distribute the liquor as evenly as possible, making sure not to create any puddles, and you need to match the rate at which you pour to the rate at which the wort is running off. It's trickier than the watering-can method, but still very popular.

TIP 52: *Improvise with a watering can*

⚫ Take the rose off your little watering can and ram it into one end of a piece of hosepipe 60–90cm (2–3ft) long, securing it firmly with waterproof adhesive tape. The kind of flexible foam-based tape used by plumbers is best because it shapes itself to uneven or odd surfaces, although ordinary duct tape will do fine. Use plenty of it – sparging water is hot! Attach the other end, using a hose clamp or an ordinary garden-hose attachment if you can find one that fits, to the outflow tap of your boiler or hot liquor tank.

TIP 53: *Upgrade to a sparging arm*

Once you start making larger quantities of beer (or if it turns out that you're not very good at sparging), you won't want to fiddle around with watering cans or even sprinklers attached to bits of garden hose. There's a wide range of automatic sparge arms on the market that can be set to allow your sparging water to flow in at the same rate that the sweet wort is flowing out, which is exactly what you want. It's more convenient, more reliable and none of the devices on the market is terribly expensive.

TIP 54: *Avoid over-sparging*

There comes a point when the very last extract from the malt isn't worth collecting. Stop your run-off at a gravity of 1006–1080. There are some nasties, including polyphenols from the malt husk and other compounds, that are extracted by the hot sparge water and are best left behind in the mash tun! The acidity (pH level) is another one to watch at this point: nothing higher than pH 5.7 at the run-off is the usual rule.

TIP 55: *Get yourself another bucket*

At every garden party there comes a moment when you've got a plate in one hand and a cup and saucer in the other and there's no table handy to put them down on. If you want either a sip of tea or a nibble on your slice of cake, therefore, you need another arm. Equally, in home brewing there inevitably comes that moment when the trinity of mash tun, boiler and fermenting vessel is one bucket short of what you require. A well-insulated 50L (13-gallon) bucket with a tap, close-fitting lid and strong handle is extremely useful at various stages in the brewing process. This is the Fourth Bucket. But you could just as well have two or three Fourth Buckets. You can never have too many!

BEYOND THE BOIL

TIP 56: How cool is your kitchen sink?

● Your hopped wort has to be cooled to 18–20°C (64–68°F) for ale and 10–12°C (50–54°F) for lager before you can pitch the yeast. You could just let nature take its course, but it will take hours, and a boiler full of warm sugary liquid is as good as an open invitation to a barbecue for bacteria and other microbes. The simplest way to speed the process is to fill your kitchen sink to halfway with cold water, run the wort into a bucket (henceforth to be known as a hop back or lauter tun) and plonk the bucket in the sink. It'll still take an age, though, even if you add some ice cubes from the freezer to the water in the sink. You'll have to stir the wort periodically to achieve a uniform rate of cooling; and you'll have to keep taking its temperature all the time. And suppose someone else in the household wants to use the kitchen sink?

TIP 57: Buy an immersion cooler

● This is a big coil of copper tubing that you dunk into your fermenter. Attach one end of the coil to the cold water tap, point the open end into the plughole and turn the tap on. Keep taking the wort's temperature and that's about it, really. It should only take around half an hour, give or take 10 minutes, to cool 25L (6½ gallons) of boiling wort down to pitching temperature, so no quick trips to the shops!

TIP 58: *Make an immersion cooler yourself*

● Making an immersion cooler is simplicity itself. You just buy 9m (30ft) of 10mm (½in) soft copper tubing from the hardware shop and spend the afternoon wrapping it tightly round a suitable former – a demijohn is ideal. Remember to leave two long ends, one to attach to the tap, the other to discharge into the drain. The trickiest part is devising a satisfactory method of fixing the inflow end to the tap: the faithful hose clamp will work only if your kitchen tap is slender enough to allow you to force the end of your hose over it, which isn't likely. (Mind you, a hose clamp is always a useful thing to have around anyway.) One solution is to wrap enough duct tape round your cooler's inflow end to make it fit a standard garden-hose attachment. The pressure required to keep the cold water circulating shouldn't be enough to blow the attachment off the tap, but keep an eye out just in case! You might well come up with a more durable solution yourself.

TIP 59: *Copy the professionals*

● Grown-up brewers often use plate heat exchangers to cool the wort, but there are also scaled-down versions on the market for home brewers. Commonly known as 'PHEs' or 'paraflows' in the trade, they were developed in the dairy industry back in the 1920s. Cold water is fed in through one inlet, which runs up and down one side of the steel plates while hot wort passes on the other. The net result is a quick transfer of heat from wort to water with a low risk of infection (provided you remember to keep it clean!).

TIP 60: Paddle your own canoe

⚫ After cooling, the hopped wort usually needs to be aerated to get the yeast breathing, particularly when using wet yeast slurry saved from an earlier brew. However, most dried yeast really doesn't require a vigorously aerated wort as it is 'ready to go' – just rehydrate as per pack instructions. The traditional implement for this purpose is the brewer's paddle, a short shovel with a narrow perforated blade, rather like a peat spade. It is an indispensable piece of kit that is simple yet versatile. Used in the mash tun, it stop clumps forming in the grain, scrapes undissolved liquid malt extract off the sides of the tun and breaks up the lumps that form in DME. It's also used to rouse the yeast during fermentation. You can get brewer's paddles in plastic, steel or wood (although wood is hard to sterilise), and if you're really serious about home brewing you can even get them custom-made with the perforations in the blade cut to your own design.

TIP 61: Use a handheld whisk to aerate the wort

⚫ Yes, we all know you can get stiff peaks in your eggwhite with a hand-whisk, but it takes forever and really wears you out. You use an electric whisk, don't you? Take the same attitude with hopped wort. The first phase of fermentation is aerobic, when the yeast cells reproduce rapidly – a practice that, as you probably know, involves an awful lot of heavy breathing – so the wort has to be well-supplied with air. When brewing small batches, a handheld electric whisk will aerate to the required 8–16 parts per million rapidly and effortlessly. Don't overdo it, though: whisk for no more than a minute at mid-speed.

TIP 62: *Use an aquarium airpump and airstone*

⬤ Many home brewers swear by a straightforward aquarium airpump and airstone as the best way of getting their yeast cells breathing after the boil. Half an hour with one of these pumps is more than enough to aerate the wort sufficiently, but there is a big caveat. Although you will sterilise the airstone and airline thoroughly before letting them have any contact with your precious wort, hostile microbes can still sneak in through the pump itself. An effective filter is therefore absolutely necessary; most authorities recommend a medical-grade inline high-efficiency particulate air (HEPA) filter for the purpose. These are widely available online, and some homebrew suppliers stock them too. The aquarium pump is also useful for delivering that little extra blast of oxygen strong lagers need to get their fermentation going: you simply attach a little oxygen bottle (fitted with a regulator) to the pump.

BOTTLING AND STORING

TIP 63: *Bottling requires a surprising number of odds and ends*

⚫ In addition to the bottles, you'll (ideally) need a bottling stick – an ingenious device that excludes air while filling the bottles. You'll also need: crown caps and possibly Champagne corks; a crown capper, either simple or fancy (tip: the fancy one is worth the extra expense); a cork flogger and mallet; and labels you can design and print yourself. You should be able to make a cradle to hold the bottle still while you stick the label on. Heat-shrunk capsules also look good and cost little.

TIP 64: *Consider kegging your beer*

⚫ Keg beer – beer that is stored and dispensed under CO_2 – is vilified by British beer drinkers, but it does have its advantages: (a) you don't need to bottle your beer, which is undeniably a chore; (b) your draught beer will last for much longer than it would if naturally conditioned in the cask and doesn't have to be drunk so quickly once it's been tapped. It does imply filtering, though: homebrew suppliers offer a range of devices at a range of prices, and filter papers that will trap particles as small as a single micron.

TIP 65: *Nearly forgot – you'd better have a keg!*

⚫ When draught sodas arrived, home brewers realised how useful the Cornelius kegs they were dispensed from would be. The Cornelius keg is a cylinder with a short inlet pipe in the lid and a long outflow tube connected to a beer tap. Turning the tap on actuates the CO_2 valve (the keg has to be connected to a CO_2 bottle), which enters via the inlet pipe and forces the beer through the outlet pipe. You'll actually need two.

OTHER BITS AND PIECES

TIP 66: *Get yourself a good set of scales*

● Accuracy is critical in following recipes, and the peculiarity of brewing is that while it might take 3–4kg (6–9lb) of malt to produce 25L (6½ gallons) of beer, the hops and other flavourings will be measured out in grams. Not many kitchen scales are truly accurate at both ends of the range, so unless you're absolutely confident and can prove, using sets of weights, that your scales are genuinely up to the job, either get a single really high-end set or separate digital scales for your hops. Good scales aren't cheap, but it will be money well spent.

TIP 67: *Keep checking acidity*

● Checking the pH level is something you should do several times during the process, from the initial water treatment right through to fining the finished beer in cask. Most homebrew supply shops will stock pH test papers, but if that's a bit outdated for you, you can get a nice shiny electronic pH meter instead. A handheld pH meter might set you back a bit but it is very good and accurate, if you look after it. Just remember, though, that a pH reading at 20°C (68°F) will actually be 0.35 higher (more acid) at 60°C (140°F) and 0.45 higher at 80°C (175°F) due to the dissociation of hydrogen ions. Therefore, a pH reading of 5.55 at 20°C equals 5.20 at 60°C. (It is better to test all pH levels at 20°C and then add the adjustments to your readings.)

TIP 68: *Avoid siphoning wherever possible*

Siphoning is an awkward and messy business and long siphon tubes are incredibly difficult to sterilise thoroughly. Whereas home winemakers must do it sometimes (because the 5L [10½-pint] demijohns they generally use as fermenters don't have taps), home brewers can and should avoid it. Even bottling is easier and cleaner (although much slower) with a pitcher and funnel than by siphoning! But if you find yourself having to siphon from time to time – if, for instance, you prefer a glass carboy as a secondary fermenter, or your test plant is based around a demijohn – one useful tip from an authority on the subject is to weigh your siphon tube down (because the pesky things do float!) by sticking a length of copper tube or even brake-pipe in the outflow end. You will also need a siphon pipe – a rigid tube that fits through the bung in your carboy or demijohn and reaches down to within a centimetre of the bottom.

TIP 69: *Buy far more sodium metabisulphite than you need*

Sodium metabisulphite, either in powdered form or as Campden tablets, is the home brewer and winemaker's essential sterilising agent. It's gentle, it's effective, it dissipates without leaving any foul-tasting (or dangerous) residue and it's versatile, having a number of uses throughout the various processes. The nuisance is that few chemists stock it, and you will almost certainly run out at some critical moment. This means making the trip to your homebrew shop, wherever that may be, or ordering online and waiting for it to arrive. So when you buy sodium metabisulphite, get lots!

TIP 70: Stock your larder

⚜ In addition to sodium metabisulphite there are other consumables that you always want to have to hand at various stages in the brewing process and which, if you don't lay a good stock in, will invariably run out at critical moments. Calcium chloride, calcium sulphate (gypsum), magnesium sulphate (Epsom salts) and occasionally precipitated chalk (calcium carbonate) are required for water treatment. Irish moss goes in at the end of the boil to help get rid of the proteins that will make your beer hazy. Keep plenty of spare yeast sachets in the refrigerator in case a starter or a ferment doesn't work. This means having a stock of yeast nutrient as well. Finings, if you use them, have a short shelf life and also need to be stored in the refrigerator. Stock lots of sterilising wipes and filter papers. Given the large number of items you'll need to stock, having a dedicated cupboard is a good idea. And make sure to restock regularly.

TIP 71: Keep it warm!

⚜ A heat pad or belt heater will be useful in adjusting temperature during fermentation if things start to get a little too cool. The belt is undoubtedly the cheapest and simply wraps round the FV; however, you cannot set a specific temperature. The heat pad is more expensive but will allow you to set a specific temperature.

TIP 72: Let the gas out

⚜ A supply of airlocks is essential. These are one-way valves that let the CO_2 formed during fermentation to escape but keep bugs out. They come in two styles, bubbler and simple. The bubbler has sections filled with sterile water and the simple has two parts, top and bottom (again, filled with sterile water). The lid lifts and releases CO_2 as pressure builds up.

TIP 73: *Watch the clock*

⬤ Get a big easy-to-read clock, either analogue or digital, to keep an eye on the time and to record the process stages accurately. An alarm clock, or a kitchen timer with an audible alarm, is also useful. Your mobile phone will have an alarm function too.

TIP 74: *Keep stirring... or have it done for you*

⬤ If you want to make a yeast starter then it's a good idea to acquire a magnetic stir plate. A little bead, sometimes called a 'flea', is dropped, carefully, inside the flask containing the yeast starter. Pop it on the stir plate and away you go. A constant gentle movement will ensure even mixing.

TIP 75: *Get accessorised*

⬤ There are all kinds of odds and ends you will need but can't necessarily borrow from the kitchen. They include: a measuring pitcher whose calibrations you have checked and can trust; a set of kitchen measuring spoons; a large fine-mesh sieve; sundry lengths of siphon tube and flexible hose, each with a length of metal pipe plugged firmly into one end; hose clamps and/or cable ties for securing tubes and piping to odd-sized taps; duct tape for the same purpose; a multi-tap hose adaptor (although they're not always all that secure – see duct tape!); a number of differently sized bottle brushes; a medium nailbrush; and an old toothbrush or two for cleaning fiddly bits. Keep them all in sterilising solution in one of your assortment of brewing buckets, although that won't make them sterile enough to use; they'll need an extra clean at brewing time!

MALT AND OTHER FERMENTABLES

Malt provides the soluble sugars that the yeast will feed on during the brewing process. These sugars are produced when the grains start to sprout, or germinate – enzymes convert the starch into sugar (saccharification) for the plant to eat while its root system develops. Brewers induce this process by soaking barley in warm water; as soon as the barley starts sprouting it's whipped into a kiln to dry, by which time the starch has become lovely sweet maltose – a feast for the yeast.

ALE MALTS

TIP 76: *Make pale ale malt your basic ingredient*

⬤ This type of malt, first produced in the 18th century as a by-product during steelmaking, was perhaps the first truly mass-produced foodstuff in world history. English ironfounders, such as Abraham Darby of Coalbrookdale, started firing their furnaces with coke instead of charcoal because wood was in short supply. When maltsters (also short of charcoal) found that coke was perfect for drying malt (unlike coal, whose tarry particulates tainted the grains) they turned to it in droves. Coke, they found to their delight, also handled better: it burns evenly and its temperature is easily controlled. Its use enabled maltsters to operate on a grand scale and turn out a perfectly consistent product. Since it never charred (unless the maltster wanted it to), it also enabled English brewers to make brilliantly clear copper-coloured beers with no hints of roasty bitterness. Pale ale malt is very versatile and has quite a high enzyme content, which is important later on. You will use a lot of it.

TIP 77: *Try using darker malts too*

⬤ The temperature at which the grain is dried and the length of time it spends in the kiln determine the colour and flavour of the malt. Mild ale malt is only slightly darker than pale, and the beer it will produce if used on its own will be a dark copper rather than deep brown or black. It will also be quite a dry beer, and British brewers usually blend a small proportion of darker malts – typically amber, brown, chocolate or black malts – into the grist for a deeper colour and rounder flavour. Mild malt is also a good base for blends of all sorts.

TIP 78: *Use darker malts sparingly, though!*

The darker malts are generally used in small quantities to add colour and richness to a range of beers – not just mild but also brown ale, old ale, stout, porter and barley wine. Amber malt is a base malt toasted and roasted to give the beer a biscuity flavour and a deep amber colour – it's even called biscuit malt sometimes. Brown malt is traditionally kilned over wood for a smoky flavour and should be used very sparingly! Chocolate malt's smooth roasted flavour and brownish-black colour with ruby highlights make it irreplaceable in dark ales; it can also be used in dark lagers. Black malt, as its name suggests, is darker still, with a sharp, burnt, acidic flavour that can take the sweet edge off some stronger beers. Then there's Special Belgian malt, which is quite a rarity and has a nutty, roasted sweetness that in small quantities enriches brown ales and porters. In larger proportions it adds a plummy, vinous quality to barley wines and strong winter beers.

TIP 79: *Use a touch of crystal for a luscious beer*

Crystal malt is produced in such a way that most of the starchy middle (endosperm) of the grain is turned to liquid during a 'stewing' stage. It is only partially saccharified before being caramelised during kilning to form sugar crystals. It's added in small quantities to ales and lagers for a luscious sweetness and deep flavour, ranging from delicate honey to rich toffee. Crystal malt also thickens the mouthfeel of the beer and creates an attractive bronze colour. If you want a degree of sweetness without the rich caramel or biscuit notes that some people find cloying, there's carapils malt. Kilned at low temperature, it adds sweetness, smoothness and body to pale ales and lagers without affecting the colour or adding caramel notes. It also aids head retention.

TIP 80: *Use wheat malt in lighter beers*

⬤ Wheat beer has long been popular in Belgium and Germany, but only in the last 20-odd years has its appeal become international. German Weissbier brewers use malted wheat, whereas Belgian Witbier brewers often use unmalted wheat. As wheat beers are generally top-fermented (whereby the yeast rises to the top of the wort), they count as ales rather than lagers. Wheat malt is also used in modest quantities by British brewers to lighten the body of their golden ales. Additionally, it helps head formation and creates that attractive lacework (or 'cling') on the side of the glass.

TIP 81: *Don't be put off by the haze*

⬤ Wheat has a high protein content, which causes unfiltered wheat beer's characteristic pearly haze. To make matters worse, wheat is low in polyphenols, which would otherwise bind with the proteins and cause them to drop out of the wort. On the other hand polyphenols can also produce a harsh tannic flavour, so their absence is largely responsible for wheat beer's mildness. Wheat malt produces a very pale beer, often with a big foaming head, and some interesting flavours, including bubblegum, banana and cloves. Its tendency to clump and clog up the mash tun means that 100% wheat beers are pretty much impractical unless you add oat or rice hulls to your mash. It is therefore usually mashed with other grains that supply a husk bed.

LAGER MALTS

TIP 82: *Use lager malt for very pale beers, even ales*

● In 1842 a brewery in the Bohemian town of Pilsen started using coke-kilned malt in the English style, giving birth to today's very pale lagers. Lager malt is kilned at a slightly lower temperature than pale ale malt, so it's lighter both in colour and flavour. Commonly grown European barley varieties contain more of the saccharifying enzymes than British ones, making them an excellent choice as a neutral base for blended grists, especially those using a proportion of low-enzyme cereals.

TIP 83: *Watch out for sweetcorn!*

● Be aware that a by-product of some lager malts is a 'sweetcorn' aroma and flavour to the finished beer. This is called dimethyl sulphide (DMS) and, while it might be perfectly acceptable in some lager styles, it is not generally welcome in ales. A good vigorous boil of at least an hour should help rid the wort of DMS.

TIP 84: *Exploit the palette of darker lager malts*

⊛ There's nothing like a cold lager on a hot day, but it doesn't have to be a Pilsner. Czechs and Germans drink their lagers in all colours, from the palest Hell through the more copper-coloured Märzen and Bock right up to the deepest-black Schwarzbier. This means that their malts come in all colours too. Vienna malt produces the full-bodied amber or reddish beers that were once popular in Austria but survive mainly in Mexico – Dos Equis and Negra Modelo are notable modern examples. Munich malt is more aromatic and yields a dark reddish-orange wort with a slightly sweet caramel flavour. It comes in two grades, light and dark.

TIP 85: *Use smoked lager malt for an intriguing iodine note*

⊛ Bamberg in central Germany is known for its Rauchbier – beer made from malt dried over an open beechwood fire rather than charcoal or coke. The rather medicinal flavour, like that of very peaty Scotch whiskies such as Laphroaig, is not for everyone, but if you develop a taste for it you'll soon become addicted. In recent years small additions of smoked malt have become very popular in strong dark beers, especially porters. Smoked malt is also a genuine taste of history: it's what many beers were made of before coke was invented. Its use had died out everywhere except in Bamberg and a handful of smaller centres in Germany and Poland until Bamberg became a place of beer pilgrimage in the 1970s and '80s and Rauchbier was rediscovered. A tiny addition will also lift a dark mild, or any darker, sweeter beer.

SPECIAL MALTS

TIP 86: Toast your own malts

● With so many types and formats of malt readily available, who would be mad enough to insist on making their own? Well, home brewing is a craft or hobby, depending on how you look at it, and since all craftsmen and women and hobbyists are to an extent stark staring raving mad – or at very least inquisitive and inclined to experiment – you would.

TIP 87: Book the oven for several hours

● Toasting malt is a time-consuming job, so make sure no one is planning a roast or a casserole. Preheat the oven to 100°C (210°F) and while it's warming up line a roasting dish or deep baking tray with aluminium foil. Pour in pale malt corns to a depth of 1.25cm (½in), reserving a few for comparison purposes. Dry the malt for 45 minutes, then turn up the oven (fan-assisted is best although not essential) to 150°C (300°F). After 75–80 minutes pick out a few of the corns from different parts of the dish (be careful, they will be hot!) and cut them in half with a sharp knife. Compare their inside colour to the inside colour of your original malt. If it's darkened to a pale buff you have amber malt. For brown malt, turn the oven up to 175°C (350°F) and test as above every 10–15 minutes. When the inside colour is as dark as mocha, you have brown malt. If all this is rather vague, it's because all ovens are maddeningly different. You will have to get to know your own oven and adjust times and temperatures accordingly.

TIP 88: *Use your own special malts while they're fresh*

● The whole – indeed perhaps the only – point in booking the oven for up to 2½ hours is that freshly made special malts have a stronger flavour than shop-bought, or at least, so those who practise the art maintain! It needs to be kept for 2 weeks, or it might produce some harsh off-flavours, but once the 2 weeks is up use it straight away. Store your malt in an airtight container and use it within 2–3 days. Grind it on the day of use.

TIP 89: *Invest in a good grain mill*

● Since special malts rarely exceed 45% of any grist, you're going to be making no more than 1–2kg (2–4½lb) at a time. Still, milling that amount is going to take ages using the average domestic coffee grinder, even the biggest of which have a capacity of no more than 200g (7oz). There really is no alternative to a proper grain mill, which are available at a wide range of prices and with degrees of sophistication, and are either hand-cranked or mechanised. The key thing to watch for is robustness, especially when adjusting for different grades of grist.

TIP 90: *Size does matter!*

● Grind your malt too coarse and you'll get a poor extraction. Grind it too fine and you'll gum up your mash tun. The ideal grind breaks the husks without pulverising them: shredding the husks will cause astringency, whereas large husks will form a filter bed that will strain the wort and make sparging easier when you run it off. So while the husks should be separated from the kernels, you don't want to grind the kernels themselves to the fineness of flour. Start at a setting of 0.9mm (0.035in) and experiment.

OTHER GRAINS

TIP 91: Define the character of your beer with unmalted grains

● Not all brewing grains need to be malted. Up to 50% of the grist of a Belgian Witbier is usually unmalted wheat, as we have seen, but the malted barley that makes up the rest has enough enzymes to convert the whole mash. Unmalted barley also has its place, either 'flaked' in strong ales and stouts to aid head retention and create a fuller mouthfeel, or roasted almost to a cinder to give Irish dry stouts their distinctive charred-wood tang.

TIP 92: Add some oats for an extra-smooth stout

● Unmalted oats, usually described as 'rolled' or 'flaked', have been heated to gelatinise their starches and contain relatively high levels of beta-glucans and lipids, which is why a bowl of porridge is so deliciously gloopy. A small proportion of oats added to the mash will produce a smooth, creamy, almost velvety mouthfeel to stouts and porters. Whole oats have to be cooked before use to convert the starch. Rolled or flaked rye is another cereal sometimes used in small quantities; it's rather glutinous and can lead to a stuck mash if used incautiously, but its subtle spiciness, especially in the finish, makes for a pleasant surprise.

TIP 93: *Lose weight with maize and rice*

⬤ Flaked maize and rice are almost flavourless but are high in convertible starch and low in protein. Used properly, they will help produce a full-strength beer with a light, dry body perfect for drinkers who like a beer with some zip but don't have a sweet tooth. They have no enzymes of their own, but as with Belgian wheat beer, the barley malt they are mashed with contains enough enzymes to convert the whole mash. They are also nitrogen diluents, which means they will reduce protein levels, and they help to reduce the 'malty' flavour or character of a beer.

TIP 94: *Make the mash more efficient and aid head retention with torrefied wheat*

⬤ Torrefied wheat has been heat-treated (like popcorn and puffed rice) to gelatinise the starch granules, break down the cell walls, and release the cereal's natural enzymes more rapidly. It's used as an adjunct for fermentable extract as it's often cheaper than malt and it also contributes to head retention in the finished product. It can also be used as a substitute for some of the unmalted wheat in Belgian-style Witbiers. It doesn't affect the flavour of the beer and is typically used in fairly small quantities of up to 5% of the malt grist.

TIP 95: *Add cereal hulls to mashes high in unmalted grains*

⬤ Oat, rice and barley hulls don't alter the flavour of the beer unless you overuse them. But they are very useful if you're using unmalted grains such as oats and rye because they form a mesh to stop the goods in the mash sticking together in one great lump. Rice hulls are also essential in a 100% wheat beer, supplying the husks that the wheat lacks. The ratio by weight shouldn't exceed one part hulls to ten parts unmalted grain.

SUGARS

TIP 96: *Use sugar for consistency*

● The use of sugar in brewing is widespread throughout the world. Some say sugar is only used to pad out the more expensive malt, and in some cases it's true. Some major brewers use a lot of corn-based syrups, and their beers are characteristically light-bodied as a result. Nonetheless, there are legitimate and time-honoured uses for various types of sugar in judicious quantities. Corn sugar is often used to adjust from mash to mash to achieve consistent strength. Beet sugar can be used for the same purpose but has an undesirable flavour that can be avoided by 'inverting' it – boiling it slowly with water and citric acid down to a concentrated syrup, which is then crystallised to form sugar 'diamonds'.

TIP 97: *Choose specialist sugars to enhance flavour*

● Invert sugar is used widely in Belgium, where it is called 'candi', to confer a distinctive flavour of boiled sweet. Like candi, some other specialist sugars are used for their particular flavour characteristics rather than as principal fermentables. Maltodextrin is a soluble starch that creates a heavier body and richer mouthfeel. Light brown sugar and golden syrup also thicken the mouthfeel, while honey deepens and intensifies the flavour of the beer (although it's best added after the boil, since boiling destroys many of its flavour components). The same applies to maple syrup. Even black treacle, or molasses, is sometimes added to dark beers in very small quantities because of its density and depth of flavour. All these sugars can be used as primers at the mash and the bottling stage.

TIP 98: *Not all the sugar has to turn to alcohol!*

● Brewer's yeast converts most, but not all, sugars into alcohol. If you're after a little extra sweetness and a fuller body there are non-fermentable sugars you can add at various stages to achieve the desired effect. Traditionally, lactose is a favourite. A sweet stout (often but inaccurately dubbed 'milk stout') can have almost 10% lactose in the grist, or a small addition of 100g (3½oz) or thereabouts either in the boil or the bottling bucket. Not much use if you're lactose intolerant though!

TIP 99: *Explore the alternatives to lactose*

● Extract of stevia is an incredibly powerful sweetener, but some brewers complain that it has a bitter aftertaste (although, it must be said, others disagree), and that it adds only sweetness and not body. Sucralose is a patented tasteless sweetener normally found in proprietary brands on a base of maltodextrin, which can taste starchy. Sorbitol is actually an alcohol and is both tasteless and powerful. In anything more than tiny doses it's a highly effective laxative!

TIP 100: *Don't use chemical sweeteners!*

● Both saccharine and aspartame have marked bitter aftertastes even in small quantities, which is one of the reasons why so many people dislike diet sodas. NEVER, EVER use them in brewing! If you need any additional sweetness, try dextrose or sorbitol instead.

TIP 101: *Try honey for a taste of history*

● Medieval Welsh brewers were famous for their 'braggot', also called Welsh ale, which used as much as 30% honey in the mash, presumably because Wales, being mountainous, is short of good arable land and grain for brewing was therefore at a premium. The Durden Park Beer Circle, that doughty band of beer archaeologists, has published a recipe dating from 1400 in which a light wort of only 1.5kg (3⅓lb) of malt is fermented and is then not boiled with hops but refermented with 500g (17⅔oz) of honey, a shot of LME for good measure, and a number of spices (which shows that in 1400 honey beer was something for the well-off!).

TIP 102: *Learn about different types of honey*

● Honey comes with a wide range of flavours and characters, so choose a type that's going to suit the beer – from clover and alfalfa for a light beer to buckwheat for porters and stouts. The amount you use is also going to have a profound effect on the beer: up to 100g (3½oz) per litre (2 pints) of wort should produce a delicate floral sweetness; more than that and the honey begins to take over until at 300g (10½oz) per litre what you really end up with is mead diluted with malt!

TIP 103: *Either use it in the boil or sterilise it first*

● Honey is good natural stuff, and like all good natural stuff, it's full of wildlife that can ruin your beer. You can add it at flame out (at the end of the boil), which will sterilise it but will also affect its flavour, or you can sterilise it yourself. Preheat your oven to 80°C (175°F). Pour your honey into an ovenproof container and put it in the oven for 10–12 minutes. Let it cool a bit, then dilute it with boiled water to the same original gravity as your wort. (Of course, you can buy it ready-sterilised, but that would be cheating!)

FRUIT AND VEGETABLE SPECIALS

TIP 104: *Make a pumpkin beer for Hallowe'en*

● The use of pumpkins to pad out the malt dates back to British colonial times, when barley was scarce. The practice died out but has since been revived by microbrewers and has become, for many, part of Hallowe'en. Some say the pumpkin adds little flavour, although it's the spices – cloves, cinnamon, nutmeg, ginger – that make the biggest difference. The flesh is generally part-cooked before being added either to the mash or the boil, in quantities ranging from 250g (9oz) to 2kg (4½lb).

TIP 105: *You can add fruit to the mash or to the secondary fermentation*

● Fruit has long been used in Belgium to lessen the impact of naturally fermented lambics and gueuzes. In Belgium the sterilised fruit – often raspberries or cherries – is usually added to the mash. Most brewers, though, prefer to add it to the secondary fermentation. You can use concentrates or purees rather than fresh fruit; if you do use fresh, you need a lot more of it – possibly as much as 3kg (6½lb) to a 25L (6½-gallon) brew.

TIP 106: *Soft fruits make great summer beers*

● Strawberries and raspberries on a base of wheat beer or very pale ale make for a tasty and refreshing drink on hot summer days. Raspberries in particular are very versatile; their strong flavour goes just as well with dark chocolate as white, and just as well with brown ale or porter as wheat beer or pale ale. Other soft fruits can also be used but their flavours – especially blackberries – are perhaps too subtle to be really successful. Still, do try.

TIP 107: Stone fruits can make an awful mess!

⚫ Cherries have been popular with Belgian brewers for centuries and are added not only to lambics but to old brown ales too. More recently, peaches, apricots and plums have also made an appearance. There are, however, two caveats about stone fruit. First, the pits or stones, if fermented, will produce methanol, which you definitely don't want. If adding chopped fruit to the secondary fermentation (the preferred method), pick out the stones first. You will undoubtedly find, unless you are a creature of extraordinary patience, that hulling sufficient quantities is a time-consuming, tedious and very sticky business! Secondly, chopped or pulped fruit behaves very badly in the FV. It willingly gives up its sugars and flavours, but it clogs every aperture it comes near and throws a pectin haze. So perhaps here is a case for using concentrate or puree instead, or you could always use a mesh bag to restrain the solids.

TIP 108: Use homemade fruit syrup

⚫ An old-fashioned but perfectly viable alternative to adding fruit pulp to the mash is to make a cordial or syrup of the fruit to add at secondary fermentation or even to the bottling bucket. The advantages of making your own cordial are: you can use up any surplus fruit your garden might produce in a good year; it's versatile and can be used as a base for non-alcoholic long drinks (lavender cordial and soda!), a spirits mixer or a pour-over sauce for ice-cream; and it will keep for up to a year. Oh – and there's no need to pit the fruit! To make your own cordials and tinctures, see Chapter 4, pages 82–4.

HOPS AND OTHER FLAVOURINGS

Some people think beer is 'made of' hops. It isn't, but the hop – the flower or 'cone' of a prolific climbing plant related to nettles and cannabis – is a vital ingredient. Malt supplies the fermentable sugar, the body and many of the flavour components of the beer; hops provide the tannins and acids that protect the beer from bacterial infection and the resins and oils that create the aroma, many of the flavour components and, especially, the finish or aftertaste.

ENGLISH VARIETIES

TIP 109: *Know your hops*

⬤ Hops can be used as whole flowers (cones), dried pellets or extracts of various types. Bittering or kettle varieties are added early in the boil to maximise extraction of the tannin and acid; aroma or late varieties are added later for their delicate flavour components. A small handful can also be added to the cask or bottling bucket (dry-hopping) to confer additional aroma. Some strains, labelled 'dual-purpose', can be added early for bittering and late for aroma and might also be used to dry-hop.

TIP 110: *For classic English bitter ales, meet Mr Fuggle*

⬤ Propagated by Richard Fuggle of Brenchley, in Kent (UK) in 1875, Fuggle became the most widely grown hop in England. Until wilt made it almost impossible to grow in Kent and Sussex in the late 1940s, it made up 78% of all acreage. It now represents only about 9% of the English crop, being grown chiefly in the West Midlands. It is grown in the US, mainly in Oregon, and also in Slovenia, where it is known as Styrian Golding. Fuggle has a typical 'English' flavour and can be added at all three stages to make the perfect single-varietal beer. It contributes all the essential characteristics of flavour, aroma, and balanced bitterness to ales, particularly as its relatively low alpha content means a high hopping rate is needed to achieve the desired bitterness levels. It is sometimes also used as a distinctive dry hop.

TIP 111: Try Goldings for a scent of Heaven.

⬤ Goldings, the other great English classic, goes back to 1790 and is not strictly a single variety at all, but rather a family of very similar strains including Cobbs, Amos's Early Bird, Eastwell Golding, Canterbury Golding, and Mathons, the strains usually being named after either a grower or the parish where they were first cultivated. Recognised as having the most typical English aroma, Goldings is often blended with Fuggle to add roundness and fullness to the palate. Goldings is also used to late-hop lager, where a delicate aroma is required, although the Whitbread Golding in particular is sweeter and fruitier than other strains.

TIP 112: Play the field

⬤ Fuggles and Goldings may be the classic English hops, but there are many others to play with. Target is one of the most common bittering hops; it gives lovely floral aromas when used for dry hopping. Bramling Cross produces blackcurrant and lemon notes and is increasingly popular in specialty beers. Try it as a late or dry hop for some very interesting results! Admiral is a great all-rounder as both a high-alpha and dual-purpose variety. Challenger adds a fruity aroma with spicy overtones and is also used as a late hop and a dry hop.

TIP 113: Add bite with high-alpha hops

Choosing hops with a higher alpha content will give your brew a more bitter edge. First Gold has an attractive lemony aroma and a higher alpha content than traditional aroma hops. It produces a well-balanced bitterness and a fruity, slightly spicy note. Progress is similar to the Fuggle but slightly sweeter, providing a softer bitterness in beers of all types. Its slightly higher alpha content suits it to recipes that demand aroma hops for all additions.

LAGER HOPS

TIP 114: *For classic Pilsner, use Saaz*

Possibly the world's finest aroma variety – certainly as far as lagers are concerned – the Saaz is a 'noble' hop that has been growing around the Bohemian towns of Zatec and Louny for centuries. Saaz is very low in alpha acids, which means you have to use an awful lot of it if it's your main bittering hop. On the other hand, it's high in polyphenols, which helps extend shelf life. The real attraction of Saaz, though, is its balance of volatile oils. It is especially high in farnesene, whose aromas of magnolia, lavender, and lemon make it as prized in the cosmetics industry as it is in brewing. Saaz is still grown in its native Bohemia – in huge quantities, despite its low yield, susceptibility to mildew, and small cones – but there are also extensive plantations in Belgium, Poland, New Zealand and the US. The US variety is higher in alphas than its European counterpart.

TIP 115: Try a blue-blooded Bavarian...

● Lager may have been invented in Bohemia, but the Germans weren't slow to catch on and the long-established Bavarian native or 'noble' aromatic varieties proved ideal. Hallertau, from the Holledau region in central Bavaria, was badly hit by disease in the 1970s and '80s and was largely replaced by Hersbrucker. Tettnang, a dual-use variety often blended with Hallertau, comes from Baden-Württemburg and is produced in great quantities for export around the world. Less well-known outside Germany is Spalt, a hop from the Nuremburg region whose aroma has been described as 'woody'. All of these varieties are low in alpha acids, with content typically ranging from 3.5–5.5%, and high in aromatic oil, and should produce soft citrusy aromas that balance the often sweetish European malts perfectly.

TIP 116: ... Or its more up-to-date offspring

● Plant varieties, however noble, eventually get tired and vulnerable to mites, mildews and diseases. In the last 30 years or so German plant breeders have been busy conjuring up replacements for the older strains, especially the Hallertau, some of which have been loaded with extra acid for improved bittering. Among these are the Hallertau Herkules, Magnum, Merkur and Taurus, of which the Magnum is perhaps the most aromatic. Polaris is another new strain with excellent bittering qualities. Among the more aromatic newcomers are Opal and Saphir, while Perle is a mid-alpha variety much prized as a dual-purpose hop.

NEW WORLD

TIP 117: *Avoid that bitter aftertaste with Cascade!*

● Developed at Oregon State University as a resistant alternative to the mildew-susceptible Cluster variety, Cascade was ready for release by 1967. US brewers, however, were slow to take it up until their regular supplies of German Hallertau were disrupted by an outbreak of mildew in 1971. Today it's North America's top variety by far. It's perfectly suited to its market: it has just enough alpha acid to qualify as a bittering hop, but not enough to produce the long, bitter finish that some drinkers dislike. But its volatile component is quite high in the richly scented farnesene, with its aroma of magnolias, and especially high in the peach-scented myrcene.

TIP 118: *Wander through a grove of tropical fruit with Citra*

● Even more heavily loaded with myrcene is Citra, which was only released in 2007 but has become immensely popular thanks to its heady scents of peach, oranges and lemon. With 11–13% alpha acid it counts as a dual-purpose variety and, in addition to the exotic aroma, has that smack of bitterness British drinkers tend to prefer. It's one of a host of American dual-purpose hops that are heavy on aroma – Amarillo, Galena, Mount Rainier and Willamette are a few others you may care to try. It's these dual-purpose varieties that have really led the charge for US hops worldwide: some home brewers believe these varieties are too close to the Hallertau they superseded to be interesting. Of course the best way to make up your mind is to give them a try!

TIP 119: Meet some fruity Australians

● Australian beers, like Australians themselves, tend to be sunny and rarely terribly bitter. Even their high-alpha hops, like Topaz and Faux Coeur (originally a French variety), are quite aromatic. Probably their best-known dual-purpose variety, Galaxy, has an 11–16% alpha acid content but is also very high in hop oil, making it potentially explosive if used very late in the boil. Australian aromatics such as Ella are bred to be both floral and full of citrus flavours.

TIP 120: Add Kiwi bite... with a bullet!

● One of the first 'exotic' hops to enliven the British microbrewing scene back in the late 1990s, Green Bullet has since become increasingly popular with home brewers. Developed from Styrian Golding, it's a bittering variety high in alphas but also in oils, which makes it very versatile – not only can it be used as the main aroma hop, it also delivers a torrent of spice if added very late. Much the same could be said of other NZ bittering hops such as Pacific Gem and Pacific Jade. The dual-purpose Nelson Sauvin is noted for its rounded fruitiness, while aromatics such as Hallertau Aroma and Motueka are packed with fresh citrus zest.

GETTING THE BEST OUT OF YOUR HOPS

TIP 121: *Use hops while they're fresh*

⬤ The aromatic oils and resins contained in the hop are highly volatile: if improperly stored, hops will deteriorate quite quickly. In fact, traditional French brewers (and many Belgians, too) deliberately let their hops go stale: they only value them for their preservative qualities and prefer to let the flavours of complicated malt grists dominate the beer. Some of them use 13 or 14 different malts in a single blend! Everyone else, though, prizes the hop's individual character more highly, and the fresher they are when you use them, the more fully expressed their character will be. Store them, if you have to store them at all, in an airtight container in the refrigerator, or even the freezer – hop aroma dissipates more quickly at higher temperatures.

TIP 122: *Watch out for cheese!*

⬤ As hops age they not only can lose half of their aromatic properties but can also sometimes develop a distinctly cheesy note. Much of this will disappear if they're boiled long enough, but perhaps it's best to avoid using hops that make you think of stilton or cheddar!

TIP 123: *Don't buy more than you need*

⬤ Before the microbrewing revolution of the 1970s, merchants only sold hops in industrial quantities and brewers generally 'contracted ahead', buying their entire order for the year in advance but having it delivered only as needed. This was fine in those days – hops were more prized for their bitterness than their aroma, so they were still good after 12 months in a tightly packed hundredweight sack (always called a 'pocket'). This, however, was no good for microbrewers, who couldn't use them up quickly enough to stop them going stale and often didn't have storage for the pockets. Eventually, an enterprising merchant saw there was a demand for smaller quantities and diversified into supplying the microbrewers. This made it possible for home brewers to buy freshly dried whole hops rather than the various processed versions hitherto available. The lesson is: if you're using whole hops, buy as few as you can, so you don't have opened packs lying around getting stale.

TIP 124: *For mixed hop grists, think about pellets*

⬤ The experimentally minded home brewer – given the tiny quantities of hops required for each brew – is likely to have several packs of hops on the go at once. The chances are that even if they're kept in the refrigerator, they're going to go stale. And they're not cheap! A lot of brewers are suspicious of pellets because they're processed, and many prefer fresh whole cones. But pellets aren't all that processed: they're just whole cones compressed into cylindrical stubs that look like pieces of green blackboard chalk. All the bits and pieces you want are there, squashed but intact. Pellets keep better than cones, though, because their smaller surface area reduces the rate at which they dry out. If you put the unused ones in a freezer bag, taking care to squeeze out *all* the air, and screw your wire closure up as tightly as possible, they'll be good for the next brew.

TIP 125: *Make yourself a hop tea!*

A hop tea is one way of adding more of the essential oils and hop character to a beer. Weigh out your aroma hops and place them in a large, clean cafetière and pour in half a litre or so (1 pint) of water or wort, heated to around 80°C (175°F). Place the lid on and leave for at least half an hour to infuse. Push down the plunger and, hey presto, you have a nice clean hop tea which you can add to the cooling wort in the fermenter when both are at a similar temperature.

TIP 126: *Try T90s in the FV*

More and more microbrewers are adding little hop pellets, called T90s, to their FVs in search of more varied and stronger flavours. These are finely milled whole hops, with some of the vegetative matter removed, that have been pressed into pellets and which look a bit like rabbit food! T90s are easy to weigh out and take up less storage space. They can contribute to a haziness in the final beer, although many brewers no longer mind this. Go easy at first and experiment on dosing levels. Store them as you would dried whole hops or plugs.

TIP 127: *Work out bitterness levels*

One of the hardest things as a home brewer is working out the right dose of hops for the required level of bitterness. Measuring Bitterness Units (BUs) is well beyond most home brewers, so you have to make do with good estimates. The simplest form of bittering calculation involves working out the AAU (alpha acid units), also known as the HBU (Home Brewers Unit). To do this you multiply the weight of hops (in ounces) by their alpha acid content. So 1AAU/HBU equals 1oz (30g) of hops containing 1% alpha acid.

GROW YOUR OWN HOPS

TIP 128: *Plant a bine*

⚫ Even if you're not exactly green-fingered, hops aren't hard to grow. In fact, stopping them growing is the problem! They're ornamental as well as fragrant, and even if you can't or wouldn't want to grow enough for all your requirements, green-hop beer is a seasonal highlight that's guaranteed to impress all your friends and neighbours. Processing and storing hops is a different question – they're not brilliant keepers, although you can freeze them – but if your bines are overbountiful there are plenty of uses for surplus cones. They're great in potpourri; swags of dried bines are very impressive traditional decorations; and dried and crushed hop cones stuffed into a pillow are a natural way of getting a good night's sleep.

TIP 129: *Give them plenty of space*

⚫ The hop is a hardy perennial climber grown from a rhizome, and it needs plenty of sun and space. Its vines (or bines) can grow by as much as 7.5m (25ft) in a single season, at a speed of up to 30cm (1ft) a day, but die back every autumn. Commercial growers build complexes of trellises with poles and wires, and if you have space you could put up a straightforward freestanding pergola in a sunny, though sheltered, position.

TIP 130: *Choose your variety carefully*

⊛ Some hop varieties can grow very high. On commercial hop farms they use cherry-pickers for the top work (once done by men on stilts, believe it or not!), although you might not want to make that investment. Modern dwarf or hedgerow hop varieties grow to no more than head height and are much easier to inspect for mites and beetles and to harvest. harvest. First Gold is a pioneering hedgerow variety and is an excellent dual-purpose option. More Due to the longer days, hops grow best in middle to southern Victoria and Tasmania. More and more hedgerow varieties are being sold, giving you a much greater choice.

TIP 131: *Use a garden wall as a storage heater*

⊛ The bines will do better still if grown against a south- or west-facing wall to allow maximum exposure to the sun, as it will act as a storage heater after sunset, slowly releasing the heat it has soaked up during the day. Plant a row of stout timber uprights 1–1.5m (3–5ft) apart and an inch or two from the wall in question to give the bines something to wrap themselves around. Secure them to the wall using wooden plates and long decking screws, and dot them liberally with wood staples to attach your twine or wiring to.

TIP 132: *Condition the soil before planting*

⊛ Hops do best in a well-drained loam with a pH of 6.5–8. They use a lot of water but don't like to stand in wet soil, so water them little and often and condition the soil heavily (so the minerals won't all leach out) with fertilisers high in potassium, phosphates and nitrogen. Your garden centre can recommend suitable manure composts and commercial fertilisers.

TIP 133: *Don't plant out until after the last frost*

● Hops need at least 120 frost-free days before they'll produce any cones, so in temperate climates you'll want to plant in mid- to late March to get a crop in mid- to late July. Time the planting to suit your local climate, but be sure to get the rhizomes into the ground only after the danger of late frosts has passed. At the extreme northern edge of the hop's climate range this should be no later than mid-May or the bines won't have time to grow, although you can start them off in pots and bed them out as late as June.

TIP 134: *Start training them early*

● Plant the rhizomes either vertically with the buds facing upward or horizontally about 5cm (2in) deep. Leave 1.5m (5ft) between each rhizome or 1m (3ft) if they're the same variety. Use plenty of mulch – bark chip is ideal – to conserve water and keep the weeds down. As soon as the first shoots appear, start training them up your lattice of twine and keep them off the ground. As mentioned, water them little but often in the first year as their infant root systems can't deal with too much soaking – they won't take the water up and will instead just rot. New plants won't produce much in the way of cones, either, although in subsequent years they can bear anything from 3.5–10kg (8–22lb) if all goes well (0.5–1.5kg, or 1–3lb, dried weight).

TIP 135: *Be brutal with the shoots*

Your natural urge will be to let every shoot flourish, but be strong! If you give in, you'll end up with a hopeless tangle and an awful lot of stunted cones. When the bine is about 30cm (1ft) tall select the two or three strongest-looking shoots and start wrapping them clockwise around your uprights. Trim any more that appear right down at ground level – get the shoots young and they make an interesting salad veg! Lateral shoots will soon start sprouting; curl these around your twine or wire and make sure they don't start tangling as they grow.

TIP 136: *Check constantly for diseases*

Hops have many enemies. Downy mildew, which flourishes on moist shoots and leaves, can affect young shoots, so be sure you're watering the soil, not the plant, and nip off any brittle shoots or curled leaves as soon as they appear. Once your bines are well established pick off all leaves and shoots up to about 1m (3ft) from the ground. If the early leaves are very dull with yellow splotches you have wilt; again, infected leaves must be removed.

TIP 137: *Keep an eye on your bines as they grow*

The bines should need little care while they're growing, other than to keep training them. Once they reach head height or a little above you should hill them – that is, pile a little conditioned soil around the base of each bine – to maintain the correct humidity and temperature and inhibit mildew. You can use slow-release pelletised fertiliser, but only in moderation. Towards the end of the growing season many growers increase the nitrogen input a little to ensure an optimum yield of well-sized cones.

TIP 138: *Watch out for bugs*

🌀 Hop aphids can infest your bines and will ruin the crop. They first appear on the undersides of leaves and must be sprayed with insecticidal soap or a non-organic pesticide at once because they breed extremely quickly. Spider mites are almost microscopic but betray their presence by spinning fine white webs underneath the leaves, which may also become slightly spotted. They like the sun and often first appear at the top of the bines, so keep a close watch. Cucumber beetles also start their destructive work at the top, where it's sunniest, and must also be eradicated.

TIP 139: *Harvest the cones when they're papery*

🌀 If the cones look ripe, squeeze them. If there's any give in them they're not ready; wait until they feel dry and papery between your fingers. The cones that have had the most sunlight will be ready first. Don't pick them cone by cone because this would take forever; instead, using a pair of pruning sheers, cut off the topmost shoots and laterals and strip them in the kitchen. Then the sun can get at the next tier down and you can cut those, too. Keep repeating the process until the whole bine is stripped.

TIP 140: *Make a green-hop beer*

More and more brewers, particularly in Kent, are now producing green-hopped ales using fresh hops harvested in September. They give the brew a distinctly fresh zingy character and a refreshing quality. Ideally, fresh hops should be used within 4–6 hours of picking and they're best added as aroma hops to the end of the boil at flame out. Don't add any coloured malt to the grain bill (100% pale malt is best), else you'll destroy the subtle notes of the fresh hops. Oh, and add at least five times the weight of fresh hops as dried cones.

TIP 141: *Go wild!*

Hops used to be grown as a sideline all over England. The hop-growing areas gradually shrank to today's two, Kent/Sussex and Herefordshire/Worcestershire, but in many districts you can still find wild hops, feral descendants of the cultivated hops of yore, growing wild in hedgerows. Give them a go; you don't know what you'll get, but it could be interesting! And picking can be a fun day out too.

TIP 142: *Store them in the freezer*

As you strip each bine, pack the cones tightly into a freezer bag – and scrunch them in really hard – tie the bag off well, and pop it into the freezer. At the end of the harvest you can either thaw them out and stick them all into your green-hop brew, remembering that the dried hops you buy are condensed from 70% moisture to 10%, or leave them until you need them. You can dry them, if you've the patience, in an oven at very low heat, but they're best used whole and fresh for a very special seasonal beer that will become one of the highlights of your brewing year.

OTHER FLAVOURINGS

TIP 143: *Spice up your beer*

⊛ Until well into the Middle Ages, many Dutch and Flemish brewers used 'gruit' as a preservative – a blend of strongly flavoured herbs and spices with antibacterial and antifungal properties that varied according to what the brewer put in the gruit bag. The most powerful antibacterial – and the most highly flavoured – component was either expensive imported ginger or its cheaper local cousin, European galingale. Hops eventually took over because they were more reliable and, being cultivable on a large scale, much cheaper and easier to source. But spices never entirely died out of brewing, and now they are back with a vengeance.

TIP 144: *Never use powdered spices*

⊛ When using spices in beer, always use them whole or, at most, loosely pounded or crumbled. Nutmeg, for instance, should be coarsely ground in an ordinary pestle and mortar; ginger simply needs peeling and chopping, although 10 seconds in the microwave won't do it any harm; cinnamon sticks should be snapped in half and rubbed briefly between the palms; smaller spices like five-spice, black pepper, coriander seeds, cumin seeds and cloves need only to be bruised or broken with a pestle and mortar. But never use spices in powdered form. The reason for this? They don't dissolve or sink, forming instead a nasty scum on top of your beer.

TIP 145: *Use a bag for your spices*

🌑 Medieval brewers used their gruit in an open-weave bag which they could easily fish out of the vessel. This is a technique still familiar to home winemakers – and indeed, it's a recognised way of adding the botanicals to gin – and it's still very practical. Whether you're adding your mixture of spices to the boil or to the conditioning vessel, a muslin bag (with a long string, of course!) is the ideal thing. Alternatively, you could make a cordial, although the drawback here is that spices (other than ginger) need a long boil to yield up their flavours and during the process many of the volatiles are driven off.

TIP 146: *Try a tincture*

🌑 An increasingly popular method of controlling the amount and strength of flavourings such as herbs, spices and sundry exotica is to make them into a tincture. This is simplicity itself: you simply mix measured quantities of your ingredient, lightly cracked, with twice their volume of neutral spirit – vodka is fine; overproof white rum is better still – store it in a tightly sealed glass jar and leave it somewhere warm(ish) such as a sunny windowsill. Shake it occasionally, taste it occasionally (for example, by adding a pipette-full or two to a measured glass of light beer), and when the tincture has acquired enough flavour for your purposes strain it through a coffee-filter paper and bottle it. Not only will it keep more or less indefinitely, but it can be used in all sorts of applications: in winemaking; as a cocktail ingredient; as the base of a refreshing long drink; as a pour-over sauce; in cooking. And the tiny amount of vodka or white rum required shouldn't affect the flavour or strength of your beer.

TIP 147: *Make cordials from soft and stone fruits*

While tinctures are an ideal way of extracting the flavour components from tough customers such as spices and grasses, cordials or syrups can be made with more yielding ingredients such as soft and stone fruits. There are two methods of preparing a cordial: hot and cold. The hot method produces a sterile cordial with quite good keeping properties (even without sugar), but the cold method produces the truer flavour. Syrups and cordials are as prone to infection as beer, so everything connected with their preparation including bottles and stoppers must be thoroughly sterilised.

TIP 148: *Use the hot method for sterile cordials*

Put your fruit in a big bowl and mash it up with a potato masher or, in the case of stone fruit, bruise it with a fork or wooden spoon, making sure to break the skin. Now either put the bowl in a *bain-marie* with very little water and let it simmer until the juice starts to run, topping up the water as necessary, or tip the pulp into a saucepan, again with very little water, bring it to the boil and simmer it for five minutes, stirring continuously to stop it sticking. Let the pulp cool to handling temperature, wrap it in muslin (or use a straining bag), and squeeze it out thoroughly. If it's for keeping, add sugar at the rate of 400–500g (14–19oz) per 500ml (17fl oz), stir until the sugar dissolves and bottle. If it's for brewing, it's ready to use without additional sugar.

TIP 149: *Use the cold method to preserve a cordial's flavour*

⊛ Clearly, if the fruit isn't cooked in any way it will preserve more of its character than if it is. However, this method doesn't sterilise and leaves your beer open to infection. So start by washing the fruit thoroughly in a sodium metabisulphite solution, then crush it as directed on page 83. Instead of cooking it, though, this time you add a pectic enzyme (as provided by your friendly local homebrew supply shop) in the prescribed quantity, mix it in well, cover the bowl closely and leave it overnight. Next day, squeeze it out as above, sweeten and bottle any that's to be kept, and reserve as much as you need to add to your fermenter or bottling bucket.

TIP 150: *Build up a collection of cordials and tinctures*

⊛ Cordials and tinctures are among the inquisitive home brewer's best friends. They're so easy to make up that you can easily experiment with a range of strengths and blends. They have plenty of other culinary applications and have long shelf lives, especially the tinctures, and they give you the option of experimenting with absolutely anything whenever you want to. A tincture of junipers will give a strong pale ale something of the flavour of gin, while caraway seeds will create a suggestion of schnapps. Then there's lemongrass, bison grass, non-poisonous flowers from your garden, chillies – anything you can imagine, all stored away in a cool, dark place and ready and waiting whenever you feel inclined to play.

TIP 151: Test-brew with extract

⚫ You don't necessarily want to produce a 25L (6½-gallon) full-mash brew every time you want to try something new. A 4.5L (1-gallon) extract brew of 1040og is easy to make up (use 480g, or 17oz, of DME) and is as useful for designing hop grists as it is for experimenting with exotic and unusual flavours. Formulate two basic brews, one pale and one dark, and repeat them exactly every time you experiment. That way it will be possible to make accurate comparisons and assessments. Of course, it does mean using a glass carboy or demijohn as a fermenter, which implies siphoning, which we've tried to avoid as it's messy and wasteful and an open invitation to microbes, but hey – you can't have everything!

TIP 152: Try root ginger for a real zinger of a beer

⚫ Traditional ginger beer isn't really beer at all, since it's made without malt. You just dissolve several kilograms of sugar with chopped root ginger and lemon peel, throw in a bit of yeast and let nature take its course. Ginger is a good ingredient in proper beer as well, though, whether it's to pep up a light summer beer or to add zing to a strong, dark Christmas beer (along with nutmeg, cinnamon and cloves, of course!). But using it is a challenge.

TIP 153: *Add a large amount of ginger to the boil*

⬤ Some brewers add chopped root ginger halfway through the boil, which they say mellows the fieriness but retains all the flavour and aroma. But they speak of using incredible quantities – 1kg (2¹⁄₅lb) to 25L (6¹⁄₂ gallons) in one recipe, for example – and frankly, life's too short to peel and chop that amount of ginger. The temptation is to compromise and use crystallised ginger instead, but that comes with enough sugar to affect the original gravity of your wort and throw out all your calculations.

TIP 154: *Save time and money – add the ginger to the secondary ferment*

⬤ By startling contrast, the amount of chopped root ginger you need if you pop it into the conditioning vessel instead of the boil goes right down to 50g (1¾oz) for a pleasantly gingery summer beer or, at most, 250g (¹⁄₂lb) for something that you wouldn't want to accompany a hot curry or chilli with! And there's always the cordial alternative: 50–100g (1¾–3¹⁄₂oz) to a litre (2 pints) of water, simmered for 45 minutes in a lidded pan (to minimise evaporation), perhaps with 300–400g (11–14oz) of sugar to compensate for the dilution of the wort, should do the job nicely. As with the tincture, taste a known amount of cordial in a known amount of beer to discover the proportions and quantities that suit you.

TIP 155: Have fun with citrus peel

⬤ Curaçao orange peel is one of the key components in the flavour and aroma of Belgian Witbier, but you'd be surprised how little you need. Recipes recommend tiny doses, ranging from 20–50g (¾–1¾oz), added 5–10 minutes before the end of the boil (the longer it spends in the boil the less you need). Homebrew suppliers sell it in 100g (3½oz) packs, but it'snot the only citrus peel you can add to beer. You can in fact use any citrus zest (the outside of the peel, without any of the bitter white pith) you want. Lemon is the most obvious candidate, but grapefruit is fast catching up in popularity. Satsuma, tangelo, even bergamot have all found their way into pale beers, and Seville orange into dark ones. Now there's a treat!

TIP 156: Use lemongrass instead of fresh lemon

⬤ Fresh lemon can quickly destroy the head on a beer. Better to use crushed or bruised lemongrass instead and add it to the FV or conditioning vessel. Remember to give it a quick douse in a little boiling water first, then add the whole lot, water and all.

TIP 157: Be sparing with the peel

⬤ We've seen how little Curaçao orange peel goes into 25L (6½ gallons) of Belgian Witbier, and the same is true for other peels. Their flavour can be overwhelming if the dosage is too high! So, 20–30g (⅔–1oz) added 5–10 minutes before the end of the boil, or 15 if your peel is dried, should be quite enough. (It actually does no harm if you dry your own peel in an oven set to very low heat.) Another 10g (⅓oz) in the secondary ferment adds to the aroma without spoiling the flavour. You could also steep 10–20g (⅓–⅔oz) in a little boiling water to add to your bottling bucket.

TIP 158: *Answer the call of the wild*

⚙ One pleasure home winemakers can enjoy which, by and large, home brewers can't, is wandering around woods and lanes gathering nature's bounty to take home and do stuff with. This is because you can make wine with just about anything, using plain old white sugar as the fermentable base, whereas beer really does need a cereal base. So for home brewers, making an equivalent of 'hedgerow wine' would imply stealing a load of barley. All the same, throughout the year there are various wild plants you can use as adjuncts and flavourings, so you need not be entirely denied the joys of hunting and gathering.

TIP 159: *Get your rubber gloves on!*

⚙ You definitely need rubber gloves, and a fair bit of determination, to get out and about in April collecting enough fresh stinging nettle tops for nettle beer. You need 1kg (2lb) – that's a well-stuffed shopping bag – to make a 5L (¼-gallon) brew, so if you really wanted to make a full 25L (6½-gallon) run you'd be picking for quite a few days. Strictly speaking, most nettle beer recipes won't produce beer at all but wine, since they recommend using white sugar as the base fermentable (at 500g per kilogram [1lb per 2lb] of nettles). But use DME (the lighter the better) instead of sugar and it counts as beer. Unfortunately, nettles aren't to everyone's taste – they're rather earthy and need the juice of two lemons for a 5L brew. But hey – they're wild! They're free! They're seasonal! Who cares about the taste?

TIP 160: *Spruce up your spring brewing*

⬤ Another hunter-gatherer option for spring is spruce, which for a few days only puts forth new bright green tips wrapped in papery brown sheaths, whose oils and resins produce a wonderfully fresh lemony aroma. Spruce tips were widely used by the early American settlers in place of hops (and the malt was bulked up with pumpkin flesh). They may well have got the idea from Scotland. It's also said that sea captains on long voyages (including Captain Cook) used spruce tips when they could get them – and, presumably, other aromatic botanicals – to disguise the disgusting taste of the all-molasses 'beer' they brewed once their regular supplies were exhausted.

TIP 161: *Make elderflower beer in July*

⬤ To call elderflower wine 'elderflower champagne' is now a crime for which French secret service agents will hunt you down and secretly guillotine you. But elderflower wine is one of the many beverages – like ginger 'beer' and nettle 'beer' – that are really just sugar fermentations made potable by any old aromatic that comes easily to hand. Elderflowers, though, are one of the most delicious of the easily available aromatics and are well worth brewing with. There are two methods: ginger/nettle beer can be made, using DME instead of sugar, or a light beer can be made, adding 200–500g (7–17oz) of elderflower florets towards the end of the boil. To separate the florets from the stalks, lay a large clean cloth on the table, take a head of elderflowers in each hand and then rub them vigorously together to create a kind of snowstorm. It's pretty! And pretty tedious, too; if using the former method, you need a whole litre (1 pint) of florets for a 5L (¼-gallon) mash.

TIP 162: Make elderberry beer in October

⬤ Elderberries are very tannic and need a long maturing period in order to mellow. A little goes a long way, too; even quite a small addition can generate a wonderful port-like depth that turns any dark winter ale into the perfect *digestif*. Some brewers dry the berries slightly in a low-heat oven before use, rolling them lightly to break the skins and adding them whole to the boil. Others push them (uncooked!) through a fine sieve with a wooden spoon, discarding the skin, seeds, and pulp, and adding the juice at primary fermentation.

TIP 163: Another seasonal special for autumn – chestnuts!

⬤ Chestnuts can be roasted and ground and mixed 50:50 with brewing sugar to make a gluten-free beer, but it takes an awful lot of chestnuts! You can buy ready-prepared chestnut chips (they're expensive) or you can peel and roast 2.5–3kg (5½–6½lb) of them yourself, although you'll be at it all week. Either way, chestnuts do add a special silky richness that makes a little effort (or money) worthwhile. A less laborious way of using chestnuts is to make a tincture of about 350g (12oz) of toasted (as light or as dark as you like) and coarsely ground nuts in a jam jar of brandy or dark rum, leave it for 2 weeks and regularly shake it, and add it to the secondary fermentation. Hazelnuts can be used in the same way.

TIP 164: *Cheat with chestnut puree*

⬤ Okay, cheat. Because an easier way still of achieving the same effect is to buy a small tin of chestnut puree and simply add it to the mash. Tinned or vacuum-packed *marrons glacées* will also do, but remember – they contain extra sugar, so the alcohol by volume will be slightly higher.

TIP 165: *Choose the right malts for chocolate stout*

⬤ Chocolate stout has become very popular in the last decade or so, although, strictly speaking, putting chocolate in it is cheating. The chocolate flavour derives mainly from the blend of malts in your grist – typically chocolate malt (of course!), amber or biscuit malt, and crystal malt or carapils. The various forms of chocolate itself don't actually contribute a great deal to the flavour but do give an earthy depth and rich texture, which is worth having. Dark (unsweetened) cooking chocolate and cacao nibs (crushed and roasted cacao beans) seem to give the best results – either 100g (3½oz) or so of melted baking chocolate (200g, or 7oz, of cocoa powder is an alternative) added right at the end of the boil, or 100g of cacao nibs in the secondary fermentation, or both but in half quantities.

TIP 166: For a coffee porter, cheat!

⚫ As with chocolate stout, an expert brewer can use the malt grist alone to create a coffee flavour. And again, the components of the grist are likely to be amber or biscuit malt, crystal malt or carapils, and chocolate malt (but only a very little). But would it really be coffee porter without coffee? Of course it wouldn't! Opt for a medium roast that is neither too harsh nor too bland, and coarse-grind the beans yourself because the coffee shop is likely to reduce them to a powder that will form an unskimmable scum. About 100g (3½oz) will do, either made up in a cafetière as normal and then cooled, or cold-steeped for 24 hours then strained and added to the bottling bucket (you can even use it to make up your priming sugars). Alternatively, the beans themselves might be added to the boil either at the very end or at the point of flame out; in which case, a second addition of 100g could be used as a dry-hop in the secondary fermenter.

TIP 167: Licorice will help the flavours linger

⚫ The use of licorice as an adjunct has a very venerable pedigree. Prescribed by herbalists for centuries to treat stomach disorders, including ulcers, it was probably first employed by brewers for its medicinal properties. But it's the natural sweetener glycyrrhizin that has the most marked effect on the character of a beer: 50 times sweeter than sugar, it has a unique lingering quality that gives the stout a rich and velvety mouthfeel. It also aids head retention. Add 15–30g (½–1oz) of dried root at the very end of the boil to get the effect – but if you want a hint of that distinctive licorice flavour, throw in a couple of coarsely crushed star anise as well.

TIP 168: *Christmas 'gruitings'!*

● To turn your favourite old ale, strong stout, porter or even barley wine into a truly sensational Yuletide special, make a tincture of half-a-dozen cloves, half a crumbled cinnamon stick, 10g (½oz) of chopped peeled ginger, a small piece of ground nutmeg and some dried orange and/or lemon peel without pith. But here's the trick: instead of using a neutral(ish) spirit like vodka or white rum as your solvent, try 20cl (⅖ pint) of dark rum, brandy or even whisky instead. Let the tincture mature extra long and, immediately before you add it to the secondary fermenter, stir in no more than 1tsp of molasses. This beer can be heated (but not boiled), although, if you do heat it, remember to replace the burnt-off alcohol with another slug of dark rum, brandy or whisky. That'll put heart into the carol singing!

MASHING
and BOILING

Okay, this is the exciting part. We've defined our aims. We've got ourselves the brewing equipment. We've studied our ingredients. Now we get down to the glorious business of heating up fluids and cooling them down, of throwing in a bit of this and a lot of that, of sloshing stuff from one big bucket to another. Yup, it's time to get wet!

WATER TREATMENT

TIP 169: *Burtonise your liquor*

⚫ Beer is more than 90% water, so let's start there. It's a myth that Burton beers are brewed with water from the Trent and that Guinness is brewed with water from the Liffey. In fact, pretty much all beer is (or used to be) brewed with water from boreholes tapping deep into artesian wells, each with its own mineral profile. It has always been said that you can't replicate a particular beer perfectly unless you use the water from its original well. Actually, you can. Brewers routinely adjust the mineral content of their mashing liquor; with a nod to history they call the process 'Burtonising'. Unless you're brewing with malt extract, which of course has already been mashed for you, you need to follow their example.

TIP 170: *Learn the difference between hard and soft*

⚫ Water's mineral content depends on the rock through which the rain that fills the wells has percolated. If the rock is impervious, the water takes up almost no minerals and is thus soft. If it's sedimentary, the water dissolves and collects various minerals and is thus hard. The minerals of interest to the brewer are chalk (calcium bicarbonate) and gypsum (calcium sulphate). They have no flavour of their own, but they affect the behaviour of the liquor and contribute to the final character of the beer. For what goes on in the mash tun is rather more complicated than merely dissolving the maltose as you dissolve sugar in your tea. There are enzymes at work in there, and the minerals can either help or hinder them at every stage from mash to fermentation. The minerals also contribute to the liquor's pH value.

TIP 171: *Learn the effects of calcium in the water supply*

● Calcium plays a huge role in brewing, from reducing pH in the mash tun to enhancing clarity of the beer by helping yeast coagulation at the end. Some 60% of the starting calcium level will be lost by the time the wort starts fermenting. Around 120–150ppm (120–150mg per litre [2 pints]) is normally sufficient for a successful process.

TIP 172: *Learn the effects of gypsum in the water supply*

● Gypsum reduces mash acidity and helps to enhance extraction. It increases the astringency of the hops somewhat, allowing you to make the most of their bittering properties. Calcium sulphate will smooth and round out the hop bitterness and works well in milds and some lagers. The well water of Burton-upon-Trent, UK, is rich in gypsum, which is one of the reasons why Burton was the birthplace of pale ales and why water treatment is known as Burtonisation.

TIP 173: *Beware chalk*

● If calcium bicarbonate or calcium carbonate is left in the liquor, it can break down during the boil and deposit limescale, which can damage your boiler. Both also reduce the acidity of the mash, thus reducing its extraction efficiency. They increase hop acid utilisation in the boil, thereby enhancing the crude bittering characteristics of the hops and reducing the amount you can use. Their ions even interfere with fermentation. In short, we brewers don't really want a lot of either of them!

TIP 174: Test the water

⚫ Good brewers should always check their water prior to brewing and then adjust the key mineral levels. Your local water supply company should have the information you need online, so go check it out; but remember – this will probably only show the average over a 12-month period. If you want to treat your water properly it's a good idea to buy a tablet test kit for alkalinity, which will show the total bicarbonate and carbonate levels. They're simple to use and surprisingly accurate. Once you know the alkalinity level you can set about adjusting it. Test the water's acidity with pH strips or your snazzy pH meter just to confirm.

TIP 175: Get the pH level just right

⚫ It's best to think of water treatment as a two-stage process: get rid of the chalky bit (the carbonate/bicarbonate), then add calcium salts (sulphate and/or chloride) to the required levels for the style of beer you're going to brew to set the pH level in the mash tun. You need an acidic mash to get those enzymes working at their best: 5.4–5.5 is ideal; 5.3–5.6 is acceptable; anything outside 5.2 or 5.7 isn't good on the whole. Remember, these pH levels apply to a water temperature of 20°C (68°F)!

TIP 176: *Use an alkilinity-reducing solution*

⚫ The removal or reduction of the bicarbonate and carbonate is the first stage. Most home brewers traditionally boil their water before use, but as boiling removes a large portion of the useful calcium and leaves sediment to deal with it's not ideal. A better way is to use dilute acids or commercial products, often called alkalinity-reducing or alkalinity-neutralising solutions. There's some complicated maths involved in doing it properly, but to take a short cut simply add the acid solution slowly, a little at a time, to your hot liquor tank and stir thoroughly after each addition, testing the pH level each time. You're aiming for a pH level of 6.2–6.5 for bitters or ales and 6.7–7 for most lagers (again as measured at 20°C [68°F]). Once you 'know' your local water it won't take so long as you'll probably just need to add 75% of the usual amount of acid solution, check the pH, and adjust accordingly.

TIP 177: *Add calcium salts as required*

⚫ As we've seen, calcium is essential for the brewing process and the two main salts, calcium sulphate and calcium chloride, affect flavour in different ways. The ratio of these two salts is more important than the absolute levels: 3:1 sulphate to chloride for a good bitter and perhaps the reverse for a mild. Calcium carbonate (precipitated chalk) can be added to raise alkalinity for some styles of lager. As a quick and rough guide:

• 1g of calcium sulphate adds sulphate as follows: 560mg/L or 123ppm/ gallon (imperial) or 147ppm/gallon (US); it also adds calcium as follows: 230mg/L or 50ppm/gallon (imperial) or 60ppm/gallon (US)

• 1g of calcium chloride adds chloride as follows: 480mg/L or 105ppm/ gallon (imperial) or 127ppm/gallon (US) and calcium: 270mg/L or 59ppm/ gallon (imperial) or 71ppm/gallon (US)

• 1g of calcium carbonate adds carbonate as follows: 600mg/L or 132ppm/ gallon (imperial) or 158ppm/gallon (US); it also adds calcium as follows: 400mg/L or 82ppm/gallon (imperial) or 105ppm/gallon (US)

TIP 178: *Salt the grist*

Add the salts to the dry malt grist and mix thoroughly. This is preferable to adding the salts to the mash because it ensures an even and constant rate of addition when mashing in and also aids solubility. Calcium carbonate is extremely difficult to dissolve and probably only 50% of what you add will actually dissolve in hot water.

TIP 179: *Strike while the water's hot*

The day before you intend to brew, treat more water than the recipe demands – say 40–45L (10–12 gallons). Run 5–10L (1–2½ gallons) off into a sanitised brewing bucket with a tight-fitting lid and keep it somewhere cool – you'll need it later to replace wort lost through evaporation and for temperature adjustment. On brewing day itself, you should have 30L (8 gallons) of treated water in your boiler waiting for the action to start. Bring it up to 72–75°C (162–167°F), which is just above the right temperature for mashing (brewers call it 'strike heat'), and you're off!

MASHING

TIP 180: *Cool it, man!*

● Stand your well-insulated mash tun (on a towel or cloth – there will be drips!) firmly on your sturdy step stool directly under the tap of the boiler. Run about three times the volume of water to the weight of your grist into the mash tun (ie, 2.8–3L [⅘ gallon] of water per kilogram [2lb]) of grist. Put the lid on the tun and wait while it cools down to strike heat. (Purists will calculate an exact temperature according to the weight of grain and the ratio of grain to water in the mash: for most of us, though, 72–75°C [162–167°F] is exact enough.) Use the time you have while the water cools to ensure everything else is ready. You can reduce your waiting time, if you're that impatient, by carefully adding cold treated water; but nature will do the job by itself in just a few minutes.

TIP 181: *Stir your grist in carefully*

● Now pour in your malt grist slowly and evenly, giving it a good stir with your paddle as you do so. You want to avoid lumps and 'balling'. Don't whisk or beat it in; you don't need extra air in the mash. A good even hydration with a uniform temperature is needed. About five minutes' stirring at most should be sufficient. Basically, you're looking to make a consistent, if somewhat thin, porridge. This ensures the floury starchy part of the grist and the husks are evenly distributed throughout the liquor. The husks help to keep a buoyant and open mash bed.

TIP 182: Secure your grain bag

🔵 Some brewers prefer a grain bag to a filter in their mash tun. It makes running off quicker and less messy, and it also makes the mash tun much easier to clean after use. Others say it gives a less efficient extraction. The bag needs to fit the tun snugly and its top needs to drape over the edges of the tun, enabling you to secure it firmly using bulldog clips (they are the most secure option, but no good if they stop the lid from fitting tightly) or a drawstring, parcel strap or even a belt. You also need a trivet or upturned bowl underneath it, to make sure it doesn't interfere with the outflow when running off the wort. Now fill your mash tun as above and stir, but without dislodging your grain bag; you need to be gentle yet thorough.

TIP 183: Use the grain bag for grist/extract hybrids

🔵 You don't have to mash malt extract – that's the point of it, after all! – but if you're brewing with extract (whether liquid or dry) and you've got a recipe that calls for specialty malts or unmalted or flaked grains, you should start your extract-based mash exactly as in Tip 9, page 16 (although of course you won't need to treat your liquor), using the grain bag to hold the various dry components.

TIP 184: Don't squeeze the last drops out of the grain bag

🔵 When you remove the bag after mashing, resist the temptation to squeeze it dry before discarding the spent grains. Many home brewers report – and there is some science behind their belief – that the last squeezings of wort produce tannic or astringent off-flavours, so it's not worth taking the chance of ruining a brew for an extra 200ml (½ pint) of wort.

TIP 185: *Make a final check of the acidity*

● Before you leave your mash to stand, check the pH level. If using test papers, put a few drops of the mash liquor onto a saucer, let it cool to 20°C (68°F) and dip a pH strip in it. The pH value you want, as with the liquor, is 5.5 (or very close to it). Compare the colour the pH paper has turned with the colour chart that comes with it. If the acidity is too high, add a little calcium chloride (it dissolves quicker than gypsum) and test again. If it's too low you can probably live with it but lower your salt dose a little next time you do the recipe. Adding calcium carbonate, which is quite insoluble, to raise the mash pH wouldn't be much use as the effort to mix it in and dissolve it will probably do more harm than good.

TIP 186: *Get the mash temperature right*

● Hitting the right mash temperature involves some very heavy maths and a complex calculation involving a number of variables from grist temperature through to mash density. However, as a quick guide if your grist temperature is between 15°C and 20°C (59–68°F) and your water in the hot liquor tank (HLT) is at 72°C (162°F) – the strike temperature – you should get pretty close to 65°C (149°F) in the mash tun when using a density of 3L (¾ gallon) of water to every kilogram (2lb) of grist.

TIP 187: *Check the temperature*

⚫ Now take the mash's temperature. It should be 65–66°C (149–151°F) and you can add judicious quantities of boiling or cold water to adjust it as necessary. Then replace the lid and add additional insulation if necessary, and leave it to stand for 60–90 minutes.

TIP 188: *Change the mash temperature to affect mouthfeel*

⚫ It's possible to change the mash temperature to influence the mouthfeel and body of your beer. The higher the mash temperature, the less starch is converted to fermentable sugar. There's a perceived difference in the texture or mouthfeel appropriate to various beer styles, which depends on the amount of starch left in it. A full-bodied stout might require mashing in at 68–69°C (154–156°F), for example, leaving some unconverted starch that will increase the beer's body or viscosity. Conversely, a light-bodied, refreshing, golden ale or lager is best mashed at 62–63°C (143–145°F) for a more efficient conversion that will create a clean, dry mouthfeel.

TIP 189: *Put the lid on the mash tun and leave it alone*

● Covering the mash tun with an insulated lid and keeping the heat in is very important for a successful starch conversion. And leave it really means leave it! There's no reason to keep taking the lid off and putting it back on, other than to check the efficiency of the mash conversion two or three times (see below). If you take the lid right off or take it off more often than you absolutely need to, the temperature will fall and you'll get a poor mash conversion.

TIP 190: *Check the mash conversion with an iodine test*

● There is a simple test for starch degradation using iodine solution, and it's worth testing every now and again to ensure your mashing regime is performing as expected. Iodine solution can be bought from your homebrew supplier. You'll need two pipettes (one of them long-stemmed), a white ceramic wall tile or a small white plate and the iodine solution. Open the lid the merest crack and, quick as you can, take 2–3cm³ ($^1/_8$–$^1/_5$in³) of wort from the mash tun, using the long pipette to reach right down into the mash. Drop it onto the tile or plate to cool. Then, using the second pipette, add two drops of iodine/potassium iodide solution to the drop of wort and mix. A strong dark blue/black colour indicates the presence of starch; reddish-brown shows dextrin; and clear yellow indicates that your wort is starch-free. However, it must be noted that just because the wort tests as starch-free, that doesn't mean that all the starch in the malt has been converted to sugar. There may well still be some unconverted starch in the solid particles, especially if the malt has been poorly milled.

RUNNING OFF

TIP 191: *Give vorlaufing a go*

⬤ The technique of 'vorlaufing' is used to help produce a clearer wort to run into the boiler. Quite simply, you collect the first runnings from the mash tun in a large pitcher and pour it carefully back on top of the mash bed. This enables the mash bed to act as a filter and take out any bits of malt that might have got through the outlet filter. Two or three jugfulls will be sufficient.

TIP 192: *Sparge the sugar from the grain*

⬤ Here comes the awkward part, when you have to rinse the last fermentable sugar out of the grain by the procedure known as sparging. While the grist and the liquor are getting acquainted in the mash tun, boost the remaining liquor in your boiler up to 85°C (185°F) to reduce the extraction of husk tannins (some add a little extra acid to the hot liquor at this point to bring the pH level down to 6–6.2 – again, measured at 20°C [68°F]). Then, as soon as you're ready to start running off your wort, fill your watering can with the hot sparging water or attach your hose'n'rose combo (see Tip 37, page 37) to the tap of your hot liquor tank.

TIP 193: *Have your Fourth Bucket and fermenter to hand*

⬤ Right. Your boiler's on the worktop and your mash tun's on the step stool. So what's the mash tun going to discharge into? Why, the Fourth Bucket, of course, which is standing on the floor under the mash tun tap acting as wort receiver. And right next to it is your FV, which is doubling today as another wort receiver. When you've filled the Fourth Bucket halfway, stop running off, slide the Fourth Bucket carefully aside and replace it with the FV.

TIP 194: *Get sparging*

● Start running off again, but this time with the mash tun's tap only half open. When the level remaining in the mash tun has fallen to an inch or so above the grain bed, start sprinkling the surface of the wort with your watering can/hose'n'rose. You need to try to sprinkle at the same speed as the wort is running out, which comes with practise. The idea is to keep the grist in suspension for as long as possible so that the malt gets a good rinsing and doesn't settle in a compact lump on the filter and block it.

TIP 195: *Don't make tramlines or drill holes in the mash bed*

● If the sparge water is kept flowing in one spot for too long or is too powerful it will create tramlines or holes in the mash bed, allowing undesirable bits to fall through or for extraction to be inefficient. Keep your watering can moving about gently and evenly to avoid this.

TIP 196: *Know when to stop sparging*

● Sparging must be done gently and evenly, so it's of necessity a slow process. But you don't want to overdo it, and there are two ways of knowing when to stop. When you've emptied your little watering can, turn off the mash tun tap. Now either take a hydrometer or refractometer reading, or taste a little of the wort remaining in the mash tun (or both!). If the gravity has fallen to 1008 (1.5–2 Brix on the refractometer), or if the wort is no longer sweet to the taste, you're there. Run off the last little bit of wort in the mash tun and prepare to boil. If there are a few litres still left in the boiler, add it to the 5–10L (1–2½ gallons) of treated water you reserved yesterday. You might need it to top up with during the boil.

TIP 197: *You could always go Medieval*

In Medieval times, before they'd thought of sparging, brewers would get two or three successively weaker mashes off the same charge of malt. Just like reusing a teabag. If you find sparging simply too awkward, you can do something similar. Run the mash tun off into the wort receiver without sparging, then pour a couple of litres of hot (66°C, or 151°F) treated liquor into the tun (remembering to turn off the tap first!), close it up for 20 minutes and add the result to the wort in the receivers. The extraction won't be as good, but it'll be perfectly adequate.

TIP 198: *Mash with half the quantity of liquor*

High-gravity brewing is often resorted to by big brewers who produce one very strong beer – 'stock ale', in 19th-century parlance – and then water it down to make successively weaker ales. Although home brewers might regard this as cheating, it's actually recommended in all the recipes at the end of this book, and with very good reason. If you mash with 12–13L (3–3½ gallons) of liquor instead of the full 25L and stash the rest in the coldest place you can find, you can add it back immediately after the boil. This has two advantages: (a) the biggest quantity of hot wort you're going to have to lug around is 13L; (b) pouring it back suddenly and splashily after the boil both aerates the wort and, if it's cold enough, will help you get a really good cold break.

MASHING LAGER

TIP 199: *Mash your lager the traditional way*

⬤ A few home brewers are now starting to experiment with decoction mashing which, although not difficult in itself, is of questionable benefit when using today's well-modified malts. The process was originally designed to help European brewers of old overcome poor malting or lower levels of grain modification. It is still practised in some parts of Germany and the Czech Republic. In other areas decoction mashing has been replaced by direct heat stepped infusion. In simple terms a portion, usually a third, of the mash volume is removed from the mash tun, put back in the boiler or brewpot, brought to the boil and held there for anywhere between 5 and 30 minutes before being returned to the mash tun and stirred in. Thus the temperature of the whole is increased. This can be done up to three times. The starting temperature of the first mashing in ranges from 15°C to 30°C (60–86°F) depending on what you hope to achieve.

TIP 200: *Know when to rest*

⬤ The various temperatures aimed for and the periods where the mash stands are known as 'rests' or 'stands'. The acid rest is made at 35–40°C (95–105°F) when certain malt enzymes (phytases) are active and break down the malt phytins to release phosphates with a subsequent reduction of pH. The protein rest is done at 50–55°C (122–132°F), at which point increased proteolysis takes place, resulting in raised free amino nitrogen (FAN) levels. This rest is important for yeast nutrition. The saccharification rest 62–66°C (144–151°F) breaks down starch. A final mash-out temperature of 75–78°C (167–172°F) is the end point.

TIP 201: *Take good, long rests!*

⬤ The duration of each rest (up to an hour) and the exact temperatures used will affect the fermentability of the wort. A full triple decoction can easily take 3 hours or more. The density of the mash at each stage will have an impact on temperature movement. An addition of hot water may be required to replace volume lost during the various boils. Add the boiled decocted portion back to the main mash a little at a time and stir it in gently. Record the temperature while doing so to help hit your target. It's a demanding process, but it has the advantage of preventing the development of some of the sulphury off-flavours to which lager malts are prone.

TIP 202: *Try a simple step mash*

⬤ A light-bodied lager needs a highly fermentable wort, but modern well-modified malts don't need a protein rest. Try this: raise the mash temperature to 61–62°C (142–144°F) for an hour for the saccharification rest, then jump it to 70–72°C (158–162°F) by adding boiling water, then rest for a further 30 minutes before raising to 75–78°C (167–172°F), with more boiling water, for mash out. Make sure you record the volumes of hot water added at each stage as this will come off your sparge volume.

TIP 203: *Take care with double decoction – it's complex!*

⚫ Now this is pretty advanced stuff, so concentrate. For the first decoction, mix your grist and liquor thoroughly (no clumps!) at 52°C (126°F), which is the temperature at which the haze-producing proteins start to break down. After 20–30 minutes, draw off a third of the mash – and make it a very stiff portion, with very little liquid and plenty of grist – put it in the boiler, and heat it to 61–62°C (142–144°F), the temperature at which saccharification occurs and the nitrogen in which two-row barley strains are undesirably rich disperses. Hold it there for an hour, then boil it for 15 minutes, stirring continuously and adding little dashes of cold treated water if it looks like drying out. Exactly like making risotto, in fact. Now return the heated portion to the mash tun, which is still at around 52°C, and give it a good stir. If you've got everything right, the temperature of the original mash and the heated portion combined will be 60–65°C (140–150°F), which is saccharification point!

TIP 204: *Okay, now do it again*

⚫ Repeat the whole process. This time the final temperature should be around 70°C (158°F); you can now sparge and run off into your wort receivers in the normal way. Modern lager malts may not actually need this treatment, whose purpose historically was to break down the grist by boiling and thus release the malt's saccharifying enzymes. But in the final wort there will always be a proportion of liquid which has not been efficiently saccharified, leaving a residue of unfermentable starches which will, to some extent, sweeten and flavour the final product and – say its advocates – give body and flavour, particularly to darker and stronger lagers.

THE BOIL

TIP 205: *Malt extract users start here*

⬤ Heat 20L (5⅓ gallons) of water to about 40°C (104°F) in your boiler, then turn it off to prevent the extract caramelising before it's dissolved. Now pour in your malt extract, stirring it in gently but thoroughly. If you're using liquid malt extract, scrape the sides of the mash tun to make sure none of it sticks. If you're using dry malt extract, stir it gently to achieve a thick consistency in which there are no dry lumps. Lumps may be okay in gravy (and are obligatory in custard) but not in the mash! Top up the boiler with water to the volume required by your recipe and bring the wort to the boil, remembering to leave headroom for the foam that will be produced.

TIP 206: *An hour-long boil is enough for pale ale*

⬤ Full-grain brewers should top the boiler up to the level required by the recipe, using the reserve of treated liquor, remembering, as above, to leave enough headroom for the foam that will be produced during the boil. But how long should that boil be? Most recipes stipulate 90 minutes for beers of all styles, but the longer you boil the darker the beer will be. A good vigorous 60-minute rolling boil should be enough for a pale ale or lager.

TIP 207: *Let your early hops steep*

⬤ There are two schools of thought as to when to add your kettle or bittering hops. Some add them to the wort 30 minutes before turning the boiler on. This, they believe, gives the oily and resinous components, which being volatile are partly evaporated during the boil, time to oxidise and become soluble, resulting in a more aromatic beer.

TIP 208: Or add the early hops as the wort approaches boiling

⬤ Many throw their early hops in as the wort gets close to or is just boiling. (Well, not exactly 'throw' – that wort is hot, and so are any splashes you make!) The hops shouldn't need stirring: the natural turbulence of the boil – and it does need to be a good rolling boil – should keep them circulating vigorously through the wort as their flavouring and bittering components dissolve into it.

TIP 209: Scoop out the hot break

⬤ As the wort comes to boiling point the 'hot break' – a grey foam-like mass of protein material – forms on the surface. Allowing the formation of the hot break is important because by removing protein it helps the clarity of the beer, but if left until the wort actually hits the boil it can literally explode over the side of the boiler. Added immediately before boiling point is reached, the early hops act as an anti-foaming agent and reduce the risk of a boil over. Another way of reducing the risk is to scoop the hot break materials off the surface of the wort with a fine wire-mesh sieve. Although not perhaps strictly necessary, it has become almost common practice and has the additional benefit of preventing the hot break material fragmenting into finer particles that might cause clarity problems later on.

TIP 210: Use an anti-foaming agent

⬤ Anti-foaming agents are generally food-grade silicon powders or gels that help prevent the boil-overs that can occur at several points during the boil. They also have the side effect of speeding up the coagulation of the proteins in the wort, and you might find – through experimentation, and depending of course on the protein content of your wort – that boiling time can be reduced from the standard 90 minutes to more like an hour.

TIP 211: A hop bag can be useful

⚫ We've already seen the advantages of the grain bag in making running off considerably quicker and sparing you the labour of scooping the hot, soggy spent grains out of the mash tun. The same argument applies to the use of a hop bag (which, for obvious reasons, should have a very long string attached!). Some say it makes the extraction less efficient, though. On balance – bearing in mind that it's your domestic kitchen you're making an unholy mess off – you might think the pros outweigh the cons.

TIP 212: A watched pot never boils (over)

⚫ Don't take the boil as an opportunity to put your feet up and watch some daytime TV. There are many opportunities for a boil-over, which you need to avoid. At first, you need to cover the pot or it will take forever to come to the boil. But the moment it does come to the boil, you need to be on hand to whip the cover off. Keep a spray bottle (an old household cleaner bottle, suitably sterilised, is ideal) full of iced water handy to spray the frothing surface of the wort should it suddenly start to rise. And during the boil, don't cover your boiler completely or the sulphur compounds in the wort that can cause off-flavours won't be allowed to evaporate.

TIP 213: Go easy with the sugar!

⚫ Any sugars or syrups your recipe demands should be introduced at the very end of the boil (called 'flame out' because, if you have a gas-fired brewpot, that's when you turn the flame out). This is another opportunity for a boil-over. Add them gently, without splashing – because that wort really is boiling! – and stir them in slowly so they don't drop straight onto the hot element and caramelise. And keep your cold-water spray handy!

TIP 214: *Add your aroma hops... when, exactly?*

● The longer hops boil, the more of their bittering compounds they surrender to the wort. And even aroma hops contain a little bitterness. For a beer with a really powerful hop aroma but without great bitterness, which is what many American brewers aim for, highly aromatic hops with a very low alpha content can be added about halfway through the boil – not the full charge, though – about half at most. The rest goes in a few minutes before the end of the boil. It's more usual in the British tradition, in which high-alpha bittering hops are used from the beginning of the boil, to reduce the bitterness extraction from the aroma hops as much as possible by adding the whole charge maybe 10 or at most 15 minutes from the end of the boil or even at flame out. Which regime you prefer depends very much on your own palate and what kind of hops you are using.

TIP 215: *Use Irish moss for a brilliant shine*

● Ten minutes before flame out is also the time to add, if you wish to use them, what are known as kettle or copper finings, also called Irish moss or carrageenan. These finings help to extract yet more protein, in what is known as the 'cold break', from the wort as it cools down in the fermenter. Not much is needed, maybe 1–3g for a 25L (6½-gallon) brew. It's actually a polysaccharide extracted from various seaweeds (*Chondus crispus* and *Euchema*). The finings come in tablet, powder, or granule form, with proprietary names such as Whirlfloc and Protofloc. Many brewers prefer them because they're easier to measure accurately and safer to toss into a boiling wort. Oh, and these last additions present another foaming and boil-over opportunity, so as before, keep that cold-water spray within reach.

TIP 216: *Using a hop back will enhance aroma*

🔘 A hop back or hopjack is a very traditional way of extracting all the lovely hop oils. It's basically similar in design to a mash tun, but smaller. In fact, you could even use your mash tun as a hop back. Fill it with the hops you choose and then run the hot wort straight from the boiler through it and into the fermenter. Some brewers line their hop backs with a very fine mesh net curtain to capture any seeds or bits of hop which might block the filter on the outlet. Small hop backs and 'hop rockets' are now available to homebrewers, so check them out online.

TIP 217: *Add a final flourish of aroma*

🔘 If you're not using a hop back, then let the hopped wort cool down to 80°C (175°F) and stir in any further aroma hops your recipe might require. Let them infuse for just a few minutes, at the same time allowing the hop debris and the coagulated proteins to settle, then run your wort off into your Fourth Bucket, which with the cooling coil in place has officially become your wort cooler. This run-off should be as fast and splashy as you can make it, since all the air will have left the wort during the boil and for the next stage – fermentation – you want as much air in the wort as possible.

TIP 218: *Cool your wort as quickly as you can*

🔘 In its current state the wort's only protection against bacteria is its temperature, which is less than 60°C (140°F). Although still hot, it may produce dimethyl sulphide, which is no longer being evaporated and will create off-flavours. It's also vital to create that 'cold break', the very sudden cooling that will coagulate some of the haze-creating proteins and precipitate them out of the wort. As well as your cooling coil, you could dunk some homemade ice packs (see the next tip) into the wort.

TIP 219: *Make an ice pack*

⬤ Boil a litre or two of water and, when it's cool enough, fill a couple of pre-sterilised plastic bottles halfway with it. Put the bottles in the freezer but, because freezers often harbour dormant bacteria, wipe them down thoroughly with your sterilising solution (not your Milton fluid wipes) as soon as they come out. Tie long strings around their necks and dunk them into your wort. You'll have to stir them with your brewing paddle at the same time as taking readings of your thermometer, which is admittedly tricky, but they will significantly quicken the cooling of your wort.

TIP 220: *Keep your eye on that thermometer*

⬤ The moment the wort temperature falls below 25°C (77°F) it's ready for the fermenter. It shouldn't take more than half an hour; if it does, you might not have had that cold break you need and you should tweak your cooling regime accordingly. And when you run the wort from the wort cooler into the fermenter, make it another good splashy one; at this stage you can't get too much air!

TIP 221: *Minimise the risk of wort infection*

⬤ This is a crucial moment, when the risk of infection is very real. You want to get the yeast into your wort as soon as you possibly can and put the lid on loosely to keep the bugs at bay until the primary fermentation gets under way. However, this is also the moment to correct any errors you may have made along the way (see Chapter 8: Troubleshooting), so have your gravity- and acidity-checking equipment to hand and perform the tests quickly!

FERMENTATION
AND MATURATION

This is when the magic happens, when all the boiling and the washing and the splashing and the sloshing come together to create... beer! And it's all down to that microscopic sugar-eating fungus (hence its posh Greek surname, *saccharomyces*) called yeast. All it does is swim around in the wort, eating the sugar and excreting ethanol and CO_2 – both of them powerfully toxic – and busily reproducing until it either runs out of sugar or poisons itself.

YEAST

TIP 222: God is good and Pasteur is his prophet

⬤ Yeast was a complete mystery until the 19th century, when Louis Pasteur found it to be no more than a fungus with a sweet tooth. Before that, fermentation was thought by many to be miraculous – so much so that Medieval brewsters called yeast 'Godisgood'. There is, of course, nothing miraculous about it – it's straightforward microbiology. Yeast has been so altered by selective breeding over the centuries that there are now thousands of strains peculiar to individual breweries, many of which keep back-up supplies in central yeast banks in case their house culture fails or becomes irretrievably infected. You can, in practice, ferment any wort with any yeast, even bread yeast, but breweries are so jealous of their own house strains that the right yeast for the beer is clearly a matter of some importance.

TIP 223: Know your top from your bottom

⬤ Brewer's yeast, broadly speaking, is divided into two families, ale or top-fermenting yeast and lager or bottom-fermenting yeast – so called because ale yeast tends to form a much bigger, denser head during fermentation than lager yeast. The terms are not entirely accurate because in both cases there are yeast cells present and active throughout the wort, but they are universally understood and are therefore perfectly functional. The two types are also known as warm-fermenting and cold-fermenting because ale ferments rapidly at a warm temperature, while lager works for up to 3 months at a much lower temperature.

TIP 224: *Choosing the right yeast for the right flavour*

● Yeast produces a lot more than just ethanol and CO_2. Different strains also produce other alcohols that generate different flavours. Esters taste fruity, phenols are spicy, diacetyl tastes like butterscotch. The flavours generated by the yeast can complement the flavours created by your malt grist. For instance, if you're brewing a Belgian ale you might want those esters; if you're brewing a barley wine, you might want a hint of butterscotch. They might just as easily clash, though. Your homebrew supplier should be able to point you to the right yeast for your recipe; if he or she can't, change suppliers!

TIP 225: *Lager yeast gives cleaner flavours*

● Another difference between ale and lager yeasts, in addition to considerations of time and temperature, is that in general lager yeasts and their fermentations are much cleaner than ale strains and don't produce as many of the additional compounds mentioned above. Lager strains are also more efficient converters than ale strains.

TIP 226: *Choose a well-behaved yeast*

What you want from your yeast is for it to do its work efficiently, then leave politely. By working efficiently, we mean converting as much of the accessible sugar as is desirable into ethanol. This is described in the industry as 'apparent attenuation' and is expressed as a percentage of the sugars digested: 72% is low, 78% is high. The rate is discovered by measuring the original and final gravities of the beer with your hydrometer. Once it's finished, we want all the yeast cells to 'flocculate' – in other words, to curl up together in clumps and sink quietly to the bottom of the fermenter. Some do this better than others, but strains that are too quick to flocculate tend to leave unfermented sugars and undesirable compounds such as diacetyl behind in the beer. Again, ask your homebrew supplier for guidance.

TIP 227: *Check the expiry date before buying*

There are many formats in which you can get your yeast, but the commonest is the little sachet of dry powder. These sachets are reliable and consistent and have a long shelf life – 2 years or thereabouts – but they are finite and you do run the risk of finding that your yeast won't start, which is always frustrating. Check the expiry date, and if buying a kit whose sachet doesn't have a separate date, buy a few more sachets as a stand-by. The same goes for liquid yeast suspensions, which are also widely available.

TIP 228: Some authorities swear by slopes or slants

● Powdered and liquid yeasts are versatile and easy to use, but some homebrewing authorities say they are, of necessity, over-processed and claim to find them a little dull, preferring the yeast slope or slant. This is a yeast culture grown on a base of dried wort and supplied in a petri dish or a test tube. Yeast slants are supposedly more 'natural' than the powdered or liquid types, having been grown in conditions closer to the brewery than the laboratory. If using them, you do need to make up a starter, and you may find the variety available is rather limited.

TIP 229: Rehydrate dried yeast properly before use

● Many home brewers – and more than a handful of commercial craft brewers – have developed the habit of scattering dried yeast straight onto the cooled wort in the fermenter. This isn't the best approach and could indeed damage the yeast. You should at the very least rehydrate it with warm water – around 25–30°C (77–86°F) for both ale and lager types – or according to the instructions on the packet. Some lager strains benefit from having a little sugar added to the warm water before the dried yeast is sprinkled in.

TIP 230: Don't leave it too long

● In general it should take no more than a hour to bring the hydrated yeast to that satisfactory condition for pitching charmingly known as 'slurry'. You will know when your preparation has become 'slurry' because that's exactly what it will look like. Once it's suitably slurrified, stir it straight into the fermenter. Don't store it once it's made up as it can lose viability.

TIP 231: *Keep an eye on wort and yeast slurry temperature*

🍺 It's possible to give the yeast a thermal shock if the difference in temperature between the wort and yeast slurry is more than 10°C (50°F). The easiest method of balancing their temperatures is to add small doses of the wort to the yeast slurry in increments of 10% by volume while stirring slowly – rather like making mayonnaise, in fact.

TIP 232: *Prepare a starter for your powdered or liquid yeast*

🍺 Powdered and liquid formats may not actually need more than straightforward rehydration, but if your yeast is to hit the ground running so that it can grow and multiply rapidly as soon as it is pitched, make an effective starter. The sooner the wort develops a dense, rocky head, the sooner it is protected from any airborne bacteria that might be floating about. Three days before you intend to brew, thoroughly sterilise a large jar; a family-sized Kilner jar, a milk bottle or a baby's feeding bottle will do nicely, but it should be at least 500ml (1 pint). Next, boil 225ml (½ pint) of water with about 50g (1¾oz) of sugar or malt extract until you have a thin syrup. (You could use some of your own unfermented wort instead.) Once the syrup has cooled enough for it to be handled safely pour it into your jar, screw the lid on as tight as you can (or make an airtight lid using a piece of foil and a rubber band) and bring it down to room temperature – or at any rate, below 30°C (86°F) – by standing it in cold water. Shake it well to aerate it, then add your yeast and close it up tightly again. It should soon show signs of life. Give it a good shake every day.

TIP 233: *Fresh is best*

● Foaming fresh yeast is undoubtedly the most satisfying to work with. You can easily culture the sediment found in bottle-conditioned beers. You could even (if your social networking skills are well-enough advanced) visit your friendly local microbrewer and scoop a couple of cupfuls off the top of the fermenting vessel – in which case, bring a sterilised vacuum flask with you to transport it in. To develop a strain of your own just skim a dollop from the top of a fermenting brew, put it in a sterilised airtight jar of syrup (see tip 237, page 126), seal it as tightly as you can and put it in the refrigerator, where it will go to sleep for up to 6 or even 8 weeks before peacefully passing away.

TIP 234: *Harvesting a crop from bottle-conditioned beer*

● If using the sediment from a bottle-conditioned beer, pour the beer very carefully into a glass, leaving 1cm (½in) or so in the bottle. Drink the beer in the glass. Then sterilise the lip of the bottle using a gas lighter, cigarette lighter or match, swirl the bottle vigorously to suspend the sediment in the remaining beer, and tip it into a sterilised jar of light syrup as above.

TIP 235: *Be prepared to fail*

● Leave your sediment–syrup mixture in a warm place (not more than 30°C [86°F], though), and give it a shake two or three times a day. It should soon begin to show signs of growth and within 2–3 days you ought to have a sufficiently vigorous culture. Prepare to be disappointed, though: yeast procured in this way doesn't always start. The yeast count might be too low, it might be a fairly docile strain, it might be too old or it might have been damaged by ultraviolet light (which is why the best beer bottles are brown). Anyway, have a standby culture in reserve.

TIP 236: Try Champagne yeast for stronger beers

● Experimenting with yeasts is all part of the fun of home brewing, with Champagne yeast emerging as a particular favourite when making strong beers. Its chief advantage is that it will continue working up to a strength of 15% alcohol by volume or more, which makes it ideal for big barley wines, stock ales, imperial stouts and so forth. And since it is intended for delicate dry white wines it has no flavour of its own and allows your choice of malt and hops to shine through. But there is one caveat: it attenuates almost as thoroughly as cider yeast, so your end product might be drier than you intended.

TIP 237: Reuse your own strain

● Many microbrewers and home brewers now try to reuse their own yeast, cropping and saving some for their next brew. This is cheaper in the long run, but only if you brew often enough – once every 4–5 days, say. The cropping is simple enough – by day three or four of the fermentation a good solid rocky head should have formed. Scrape off the top crust with a sterile spoon then carefully scoop out 3–4tbsp of dense yeast slurry. Pop it all into a sterile container and keep it in the bottom of a cold refrigerator, preferably at below 5°C (41°F).

TIP 238: *Be an acid bath murderer (of bacteria, that is)*

⬤ But cleanliness and sterility are paramount. If you suspect a bacterial infection of your yeast – if it smells sour or slightly vinegary – and it happens to be the only yeast you have, give it an acid bath. You need a strong solution of acid, usually phosphoric, at a concentration of 7.5–10% in strength and with a pH of 2–2.1. Chill both the acid and the yeast down to below 5°C (41°F). Add the acid solution slowly, a little at a time, to the yeast slurry while stirring continuously. Measure the pH after stirring in each addition of acid. When it's ready, pitch the whole lot in one go straight into the fermenter.

TIP 239: *Go 'turbo' with your yeast*

⬤ In recent years, and especially in America, some home brewers have been experimenting with distillers and so-called 'turbo' yeasts. Like Champagne yeast, they're tolerant to high levels of alcohol, and they're also tolerant of high temperatures, which makes them useful if you don't have a cool place for your fermenter or you're brewing in a heatwave (or in the tropics). The speed at which these yeasts work, though, has been credited by some with producing some pretty undesirable off-flavours! Perhaps worth a try, but don't be too disappointed with an unsatisfactory result.

FERMENTATION

TIP 240: *Make a little whirlpool*

🌑 It's time now to run the hopped wort into the FV. First, take the cooling coil out of the wort cooler. Then with your paddle give enough mighty swirls to cause an eddy or, to be grand, a whirlpool. When this subsides you will find, by the magic of physics, that any bits of hop leaf and coagulated protein that managed to get from the boiler's filtration system into the wort cooler will have been scooped up together and (should) have sunk to the bottom of the cooler. You may now run the clear and debris-free hopped wort into the FV.

TIP 241: *Whip out the old hydrometer*

🌑 As soon as you've run the hopped wort into the FV, take its gravity with your hydrometer and record it in your brewing book. You'll be recording its fall every day for the next 4–5 days until it comes as close to 1000 as is feasible, at which point you'll be racking it off for its secondary fermentation. If the gravity suddenly stops falling, you've probably got a stuck fermentation – in which case, see Chapter 8, Troubleshooting, page 187. If the original gravity is too high, bring it down using your reserve of treated water.

TIP 242: Take the wort's temperature

⚙ It's very important at this stage to ensure that your wort has cooled to 30°C (86°F) or a little below. Above that, and the take-up of air in the next operation will be insufficient to get the yeast going. If it's still too warm, and you don't want to add any more of your reserve of treated water because the original gravity is where you want it, revert to the old plastic-bottle-of-ice trick described in the previous chapter.

TIP 243: Give the wort some air

⚙ Yeast works in two distinct stages. The primary or aerobic fermentation is the spectacular one that throws the thick frothy head; at this stage the yeast is not producing alcohol but is guzzling sugar in order to multiply, and it needs plenty of air to help in the process. A lot of heavy breathing goes on during reproduction, in yeast as in other species! This is why wort has to be thoroughly aerated and why yeast cultures in preparation must be both shaken and stirred. Failure to aerate can lead to a stuck fermentation. Once the aerobic phase has come to an end, the yeast population will have multiplied sufficiently to enter phase two, anaerobic fermentation, when the alcohol is produced and air must as far as possible be excluded.

TIP 244: Make a splash

⚙ To aerate even more thoroughly, run a few litres of wort into one of your buckets, swirl it as vigorously as possible a few times, and then tip it back into the FV from a height. Repeat this procedure two or three times and you should have introduced enough air for the yeast to work on. A few good stirs with your paddle will aid the process and then, if you wish, you can introduce the aquarium pump (see Tip 62, page 42) and let it run for half an hour.

TIP 245: *Use more yeast for lagers and strong beers*

The amount of dried yeast you use is rarely a critical question. The rule of thumb is simple: one 25g (⁴⁄₅oz) dose, be it powdered, liquid or fresh, will ferment 25L (6½ gallons) of wort whose original gravity is the usual 1.050 or thereabouts. The much denser worts that will become strong ales, barley wines and so forth should have a proportionately higher yeast count if they're to get started equally quickly (the sooner they start, the less prone they are to infection), so pitch with a double dose. The same goes for lager; the lower temperature of the ferment slows the yeast's reproduction rate, so a big initial dose will speed matters up (see Fermenting Lager, page 137).

TIP 246: *Distribute the yeast evenly*

So at last it's time to introduce your yeast starter to your wort. This is the magic moment of brewing, so you might want to make a bit of a ritual of it. Don't just slosh the starter straight in; distribute it as evenly as possible throughout the wort by pouring it slowly across as much of the surface of the liquid as possible. Then give the wort a thorough stir with your paddle – not too vigorous, but thorough and deliberate.

TIP 247: *Feed the yeast*

Sugar is yeast's delight, but refined sugars lack the trace minerals that our little fungal friend also requires. Full mash and all-malt extracts can supply everything the cells need to reproduce, but any recipe that calls for additional white sugar or corn syrup – and this includes some kits – will leave the yeast hungry for nitrogen, amino acids, zinc, magnesium and other minerals. These deficiencies are often the cause of stuck ferments, but homebrew suppliers all stock proprietary brands of yeast nutrient. It's important to follow the instructions on the packet.

TIP 248: *Keep a lid on it*

⊙ So far we've avoided having to hoist a 30–40kg (90lb) bucket of liquid around, but now it's inevitable. So give it one last stir for luck and, to protect it from infection while the yeast reproduces, pop the lid on (although not too firmly!). Some of these brewing buckets have lids that are extremely difficult to remove. Now carefully move your FV from the step stool to its final resting place, preferably one with a stable temperature – a garage may be too cold in winter, and a kitchen or bedroom too warm in summer. You are now awaiting the formation of the head, a period known to brewers as 'lag time'. This should only take 24–48 hours; if there's no sign of a head after 2 days, consult the Chapter 8, Troubleshooting, page 187.

TIP 249: *Keep a close eye on the head*

⊙ Once the initial fluffy head forms, carefully scoop out any dark flecks and bits of hop (not that there should be any!) with a slotted spoon; you don't actually need to replace the lid, but it's probably wise. If the fermentation is taking place in the cupboard under the stairs, there's always the risk of bits of plaster, dead spiders and other nasties falling into it; if it's in the kitchen, there are always tiny droplets of airborne grease and other cooking by-products floating about which you don't really want in your beer. But a vigorous early fermentation should be producing enough CO_2 at this point to poison most of the alien microbes that may come calling.

TIP 250: *If it feels right, skim it*

⬤ On an ale or stout you should very quickly get a head which is invariably described as 'dense and rocky'. If the head is so dense and rocky that it's threatening to overspill the top of the FV, simply skim it with a perfectly ordinary (but sterilised!) slotted spoon. You might also want to give it a skim towards the end of primary fermentation, when the head might be in danger of collapsing into the beer. Otherwise it's not really necessary and you probably ought to leave well alone. But stand your FV on a good absorbent mat or towel anyway, just in case.

TIP 251: *Get into a routine*

⬤ During the first stages of fermentation it's important to check the temperature and take a hydrometer reading every day. It is a good idea to do it at the same time every day because you get more closely comparable results and also because you're less likely to forget. Two things to bear in mind here: first, fermentation is an endothermic reaction, which means it generates heat. Your cupboard, kitchen or garage may be at the optimum temperature (18–22°C [65–72°F] for ale and 7–12°C [45–55°F] for lager) but the temperature in the FV could be as much as 10°C (50°F) higher. In that case you're in trouble and need to act – the ice-in-soda-bottle trick should do it. Second, the gravity should fall every day as the yeast munches its way through the sugar. If it stops falling before it ought to, you probably have a stuck fermentation (See Chapter 8, Troubleshooting, page 187). But if it's fallen to roughly where you expected it to and activity seems to have ceased, then you're ready for the next step.

TIP 252: *Give it a rest*

● Some people like to get their beer into the secondary fermenter as soon as the primary fermentation has definitely stopped. Others prefer to give it a day or two's rest in a holding tank (another job for the Fourth Bucket!) to allow excess yeast to settle out. This makes for a little extra work, but it does lead to a more refined beer without that bready 'homebrew' taste. Alternatively, just leave the beer in the FV for a couple of days after fermentation has stopped.

TIP 253: *Choose the most suitable secondary fermenter*

● For cask-conditioned ales, the secondary fermenter will also be the vessel you dispense from. This is, after all, the meaning of cask conditioning! A simple polycask fitted with a self-venting pressure cap will do the job nicely, although it isn't exactly decorative. Fancier (and much more costly) pressure barrels are available. The key thing is not to move it once it's ready to drink, or its sediment will have to settle all over again, so choose the right place for the job. With lagers or any beer that you intend to keg, use a brewing bucket (with tap installed) rather than a polycask, because you're going to have to chill it again and your chiller won't fit into a barrel!

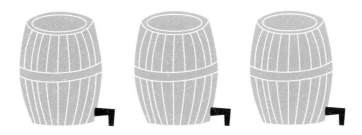

SECONDARY FERMENTATION OF ALE

TIP 254: *Get ready to rack!*

⬤ Racking, or transferring, into the secondary fermenter needs to be done with some care, because oxygen is no longer welcome. Attach a weighted tube to the tap of your FV (or holding tank, if you're using one) to make sure the weighted end actually rests on the base of the receiving vessel and remains below the surface of the liquid during the run-off. Fill the secondary fermenter right up – the vent in the screw-top will prevent it from exploding – and seal it as tightly as you can. If it isn't quite full when you rack your beer into it, it should be vented after 2 days. This will allow the air in the headroom to be expelled and replaced by the CO_2 given off by the slight residual fermentation that will be going on.

TIP 255: *Have it the British way*

⬤ British beer-drinkers – or those who know their beer – generally prefer their draught ale 'cask-conditioned'; that is, still slowly working away in the vessel from which it is dispensed. The principal advantage of this dispensing method is that it's the least processed and most unmucked-about-with of all possible formats – the beer is exactly as you intended it, with all the characteristics and properties you imbued it with still completely intact. Another advantage is that the carbonation is always much lower than American or Australian beer-drinkers are used to, which – combined with the fact that it's meant to be served at 10–12°C (50–54°F) (not 'warm'!) – means you can drink it really quickly. Which is perhaps why a British session bitter is usually below 4% ABV and mild can be as low as 3.2%.

TIP 256: *Simply dry-hop and prime it*

● There's no need to filter, pasteurise or carbonate cask-conditioned beer; simply dose it with 40–50g (1½oz) of aroma hops (or whatever the recipe requires) and add in the same priming sugars you'd normally use in the bottling bucket, then seal your pressure-cask nice and tight and leave it alone in a cool, dark place. Untapped (and provided the storage temperature is even), it will keep for weeks or even months; a strong beer of 7% ABV or above might even keep for years. If you can leave it alone that long, that is!

TIP 257: *More tea, Vicar?*

● Well, you might feel you've earned a nice cup of tea after all that, but that's not what's going on here. Remember that anything going into the barrel has to come out if it. As things stand that includes a good handful of soggy hops, which might be quite stubborn about being removed. Fear not! There is an easier alternative – make another hop tea. Sterilise a cafetière, swill it with boiling water until it's nice and hot, throw in your aroma hops and also, this time, your priming sugar, add boiling water and give it the usual half an hour before pressing the plunger. Add that to the barrel and, hey presto, dry-hopping without tears!

TIP 258: *Leave stronger ales for longer*

How long should a cask ale be left before you tap it? Well, how long is a piece of string? A mid-strength beer will benefit from at least 2 weeks' secondary fermentation; a stronger beer should be aged for even longer before it reaches its peak – 3–4 weeks, say, for an ale of 4.5–6% ABV; and some impossibly strong beers will keep on improving almost indefinitely. If you store them in optimum conditions and can resist the temptation to tap them, even session-strength beers will keep for 2–3 months, strong beers for up to 6 months and very strong beers. Well, there's no knowing.

TIP 259: *Waste not...*

Cask-conditioned beer's great drawback is that once you've tapped it you have 4 days at most in which to drink it; so invite a lot of friends round! But if they can't quite polish it off you can reprieve the leftovers for a few more days by running them off into a collapsible polypin (a strong polythene bag with a tap), squeezing any air out as you do so; but still, they won't keep long. (An old British publican's trick is to revive a slightly tired cask by pouring in a bottle of ginger ale – not diet, though, because it's the sugar that supposedly does the trick. It's not recommended, though, because it doesn't really work.) Alternatively, recycle any surplus by bottling it with a little fresh primer, or even by adding it back to the secondary fermentation of whatever else you've got on the go. Unorthodox, but better than throwing it away.

FERMENTING AND CONDITIONING LAGER

TIP 260: Don't worry about the smell!

● Lager yeasts work more slowly than ale yeasts. As we have seen, that means using a double dose to get the aerobic phase out of the way as quickly as possible. During the first fermentation lager strains also produce sulphur compounds that stink of rotten eggs. Don't worry about it, though; the secondary fermentation will get rid of the sulphur and its diabolical smell.

TIP 261: Cool the wort quickly

● Lager strains also work at a lower temperature than ale and stout yeasts, and it's essential to get the wort down to pitching temperature as soon after the boil as possible. Warm wort is a laboratory for all sorts of reactions that will produce off-flavours, and as one of the virtues of any lager is its clean flavour you want to get that yeast working as rapidly as you can. The ideal pitching temperature for the wort is 10–12°C (50–54°F), so get that cooler out and have those ice bottles handy! Cool your yeast starter, too. Get it into the refrigerator the night before and let it drop to about 5°C (41°F).

TIP 262: Give the yeast a hearty breakfast

● Another way to get the yeast going quickly is to feed it the two menu items it likes best at this stage: oxygen and protein. Your aquarium air pump, used for half an hour, is fine for ale but delivers less than half the oxygen lager requires. A 5-minute squirt from a small oxygen tank via the aquarium pump will raise the oxygen level to 25ppm, which is ideal. Add all-purpose nutrient, including a nitrogen supplement, yeast hulls, vitamins and minerals, and your fermentation should get off to a flying start.

TIP 263: *You can let the wort warm up, but only a little*

⚫ Holding the temperature of the wort down to 7°C (45°F) throughout the 3–5 weeks (yes, that long!) of primary fermentation in a modern, heated home is quite a challenge. Even the garage is likely to be warmer than that, and to complicate matters further the furiously reproducing yeast cells will be generating a fair bit of warmth of their own, as tends to happen when one reproduces furiously. The consensus is that it doesn't do too much harm to let the temperature rise to 11–12°C (52–54°F) or so. Keep taking its temperature and don't be afraid to deploy the ice bottles if necessary.

TIP 264: *Rack it as soon as it slows down*

⚫ The primary fermentation of a lager can be surprisingly turbid, throwing a head that is not perhaps as dense as that of an ale or stout but every bit as dramatic. The right time for racking into the secondary fermenter (or lagering tank, as we should now call it) is a matter of personal judgement, but once the hydrometer reading shows the beer is about three-quarters of the way to its final gravity, a good rule of thumb is to watch out for the head showing signs of collapsing into the beer. That's when you want to run it off.

TIP 265: *Keep it wintry*

⚫ Before mechanical refrigeration, lager went through its secondary fermentation or 'lagering' in glacial Alpine caves. Now it's your turn to wish you had an icy cavern of your own! From the 11–12°C (52–54°F) of primary fermentation you need to get the beer down to 2°C (36°F) and hold it there for up to 2 months. You can get away with lagering for 4–5 weeks at 7°C (45°F), but the point of the long, cold regime is to coagulate any last bits of protein that might cause a chill haze. So opt for as long and cold as you can.

TIP 266: *Rescue an old refrigerator*

⬤ At a pinch, and with constant monitoring, you can lager your beer in a well-insulated box packed with bags of ice, but it's a pesky business. No, the best way to ensure you're lagering at the correct temperature is the obvious one: do it in a second-hand refrigerator. Maybe you know someone who's getting rid of one, or maybe your municipal dump is overwhelmed with the damned things (which are a nightmare to recycle – they'll probably be glad to get rid of one!). The key thing, though, is consistency, so if you're feeling rich, splash out on an automatic temperature controller. Not an awful lot of money well spent!

TIP 267: *Use beechwood curls to speed up the process*

⬤ To make Budweiser, Anheuser-Busch uses 1m (3ft) lengths of beechwood, boiled in baking soda for several hours, to speed up the lagering process. Instead of sinking to the bottom in a clump the yeast cells collect on the surface of the wood, increasing the area of contact between yeast and beer and so making the yeast more efficient. Beechwood is favoured because it's low in resins and oils and shouldn't affect the flavour of the beer. You too can use it, in the form of curls dunked into the secondary fermenter using your grain bag, to brighten and clear the beer before it goes into the keg.

FINING

TIP 268: Fine your beer for clarity

⬤ Cask fining is the process of clearing the beer of microscopic particles of yeast by adding an agent such as natural collagen (isinglass, derived from the swim-bladders of fish) or unflavoured gelatine. Isinglass is positively charged and attracts the negatively charged yeast particles as it slowly settles through the beer. Gelatine is easier to use but less effective, with only about a tenth of the power of isinglass. But is fining really necessary? Fining was adopted by commercial brewers whose beers faced a long and often bumpy ride from brewery to bar and stood a better chance of clearing if they were fined first. Also, customers have come to expect a crystal clear pint. As your beer won't face ordeal either by brewer's dray or by beer bore, you might not want to fine it at all. Indeed, there's now an emerging trend for unfined cask ales.

TIP 269: A vegetarian alternative

⬤ Isinglass and gelatine are both animal derivatives, meaning that beer in which they've been used isn't vegetarian. A fish had to give its life so that your beer might sparkle, and you might feel that the result wasn't worth the slaughter (although as isinglass is a by-product, not using it won't save a single piscine life; it'll just mean that Vietnamese fishermen get less for their catch). Bentonite, a form of clay, is the most common alternative. But Bentonite acts on protein rather than yeast, which is what you're trying to get rid of here, and is also very messy. Better, perhaps, are the various silicone gels on the market, although they may not be the most environmentally kind alternatives.

TIP 270: *There will be times when fining is necessary*

You promised to supply the beer for your daughter's wedding. With 10 days to go you haven't got round to it yet. Quick, brew! But wait! There's no time to age the beer; you need to fine it! Well, it could happen. More likely, though, is that you're not 100% confident and you just want to be sure your beer is bright and beautiful. You can buy isinglass either as a ready-to-use liquid or a pre-hydrolysed powder. The powder needs to be made up to double its volume with some of your beer; a total volume of 150–250ml (5–8½fl oz) should be enough for a 25L (6½-gallon) brew. The tricky bit is adding it. By now, your beer is in a cask with a narrow opening, but the isinglass needs to be distributed evenly and yet you need to keep the air out of the beer. Simple: pour in the dose of isinglass, seal the cask firmly and roll it along the floor a couple of times.

TIP 271: *You could just let the beer grow old gracefully*

A better choice is to allow the surviving yeast time to munch its way gradually through any remaining carbohydrates in the beer and then, having joined the choir invisible and shuffled off this mortal coil, sink slowly to the bottom of the cask. A session-strength beer of around 1040og should 'drop bright' (another nice bit of brewing jargon for you) all by itself in a couple of weeks and will be all the better for the opportunity to mature at its own pace.

SOUR BEERS

TIP 272: *Infect your beer with bacteria*

⬤ You might think sour beer is a bad thing, but plenty of people love a Berliner Weisse, an oud bruin or a gueuze, which are all deliberately soured using bacteria. One of these, delbrueckii, is a harmless probiotic that is also used to sour yoghurt. The other, pediococcus, is used to ferment sauerkraut and farm silage. Although these bacteria aren't yeast, they are made up as a starter with sugar or DME and normally pitched during or immediately after the primary fermentation. They digest simple sugars such as glucose and give off lactic acid, which is what gives these beers their tang. Pediococcus can also produce the butterscotch-flavoured diacetyl.

TIP 273: *Go easy on the hops*

⬤ Anything more than 10 units of bitterness will destroy the lactobacillus culture, so making a sour beer starts with the boil. Use a strain suitably low in alpha acids – and don't use too much!

TIP 274: *You will still need yeast*

⬤ Being bacteria, lactobacilli don't produce alcohol. In fact, by competing with the yeast for simple sugars they can reduce the final strength of your beer. In commercial preparations, whether slopes or liquids, lactobacilli are blended with saccharomyces and often with brettanomyces as well; some enthusiasts use them with brettanomyces alone. If using a commercial preparation, keep the primary fermentation temperature at 19–21°C (66–70°F) so the yeast can establish itself before the lactobacilli get going.

TIP 275: Handle with care

⬢ Handle the bacteria with care, not because they're dangerous, but because they're awkward to use. The starter, for instance, can take 4 days to work itself up to pitching strength and needs to be kept at above room temperature – 22–23°C (72–73°F) – all that time, so you might need a winemaker's warming pad. If you're not using a commercial blend but a pure lactobacillus, you're advised not to add it until the primary fermentation is all but complete, in order to give the yeast a chance. And if the pH value of the fermenting wort is allowed to fall below 4.0, the lactic acid can produce an overwhelming, pervasive and persistent smell of sour milk which doesn't affect the taste of the beer but does rather spoil the pleasure of drinking it!

TIP 276: Go wild with brettanomyces

⬢ The lambic brewers of Payottenland near Brussels not only leave their fermenting beer uncovered, they throw open the louvred ceilings of their breweries and invite the passing microbes in. The precise ecology of each brewery is different, and the brewers themselves refuse to change a thing, even daring to tangle with the health and safety police because they profess not to know what's what and what does what; and they don't want to upset a balance of microflora and microfauna that has developed naturally. But whatever's hiding in the undergrowth of each brewery's jungle, the king of the Belgian beasts are the yeasts *Brettanomyces bruxellensis* and *lambicus*, which are both available for you to buy.

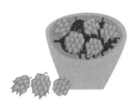

TIP 277: *Keep it simple – use a prepared culture*

🌑 You can culture your own brettanomyces strain, and some do, but it takes years and is a complicated business since brettanomyces is very choosy about what it eats. Better to buy a prepared culture that you add once the primary fermentation is over. It's a slow grower and can convert complex sugars that saccharomyces turns it nose up at. Brettanomyces doesn't excrete a lot of alcohol, but it does produce various ethyls that give lambic beers their, err, farmyard notes. If using a prepared culture, you can use it in the primary fermentation but the same rules remain in force: ensure a low hop bitterness and low fermenting temperature.

TIP 278: *Be prepared for a long, long wait*

🌑 Both lactobacilli and brettanomyces are slow developers – very slow developers, in fact, meaning that brewing sour beers is not for the impatient. Brettanomyces-based beers can take anything up to 18 months before they are ready to bottle; certainly no sour beer that you're starting to mash in today will be drinkable for 8 months. On the other hand they are great keepers and can be good after years in bottle, and even if you don't love them for themselves they make great blenders with all sorts of other beers and ingredients – notably, of course, cherries and raspberries.

BEER FROM THE WOOD

TIP 279: *Don't be afraid of the woods*

◉ Breweries – they're all gleaming stainless steel and ultra-hygienic plastic these days. The only wood you see anywhere is a few preserved beer barrels as a reminder of the old days and, of course, the mirror-like mahogany table in the boardroom. But it's not much more than half a century ago that almost all beer was fermented and matured in wood. And now it's making a comeback: first craft brewers and now home brewers are increasingly looking for the extra flavour and character they can get by using oak barrels.

TIP 280: *Oak barrels aren't as hard to find as you'd expect*

◉ Although the once-ubiquitous brewery cooperage has (with a handful of honourable exceptions) pretty much died out, there's no shortage out there of people still making and repairing barrels. Mainly you'll find them in the wines and spirits industries in North America, Scotland, France and Spain; but even their smallest barrels might be a bit big for all but a handful of home brewers. There are, however, many small commercial cooperages whose bread and butter has been making ornamental barrels as bar decorations and garden planters but which also make practical, usable beer and wine barrels ranging from 30–100L (8–26 gallons) and either of oak or chestnut. They aren't even terribly expensive!

TIP 281: *Used is best*

⬤ Assuming that you're making enough beer to justify buying a discarded wine or spirit cask, you're in for a treat. New oak is very tannic and can create bitter off-flavours until it's been used once or twice. But old whisky, brandy and rum casks, if you can get them, used as conditioning vessels can still surrender enough of their original occupants' flavours to round out and enrich almost any beer in a most delightful way. Whisky barrels are commonplace in the United States, where the law only allows casks to be used once. Unfortunately, wines and other spirits tend to be bottled at the point of origin these days rather than shipped in barrels, as used to be the case. But they're still around, and the internet has made them easier to find.

TIP 282: *Sour beers love oak*

⬤ Sour beers such as lambics and oud bruins seem to have a particular affinity for oak. There are many reasons for this, not least being that as they are very low in bittering hops they are naturally short of tannin, and what they extract from the oak makes up for the deficiency. The tannin makes up for the lack of alpha acids in another important way, too: it protects against bacteria. Another is that sour beers, like fine red wines, take a long time to mature – as long as 18 months in some cases – and during the process much of the tannin's astringency disappears, leaving behind desirable oak-derived flavour components such as vanillin. So, if you're using lactobacilli or brettanomyces, why not use oak as well?

TIP 283: *Mature an old ale or stock ale in new oak*

⬤ If you like the idea of fermenting in wood but you're not crazy about sour beer, try using new oak to mature old ale or stock ale, and for the same reasons. Rein back a little on the bittering hops, or use all aroma varieties; the oak's own tannin will compensate. And let the ale spend a year in the cask so the tannin can break down and the vanillin can shine through. You should end up with a real Burgundy of a beer!

TIP 284: *A barrel on its side makes a great lagering tank*

⬤ Everybody thinks lager has to condition in an upright cylindro-conical tank, but well within living memory lagers were conditioned in horizontal tanks, often of oak. The Pilsner Urquell brewery had a particularly large set that, when cylindro-conicals were installed, were converted into holiday chalets! But modern upright fermenters attenuate more fully than old-fashioned horizontals, making the horizontal the ideal alternative when you want a slightly richer beer – a Vienna or a Märzen, say. The fact that the barrel has a conveniently placed tap makes the run-off easier, too, and the bung-hole at the top is perfect for an airlock.

TIP 285: *A barrel makes a fine FV too*

🌑 So far we've talked about barrels being used for the long, slow secondary fermentation of special beers. But an upended barrel with its head taken off – and used in the earliest stage as a loose lid – makes a fine open FV. Leave plenty of headspace, though; the surface area may be less than what you're used to, which means the head will be deeper – and you don't want it all over the kitchen floor.

TIP 286: *Use broken-in barrels for session ales*

🌑 Britain's Society for the Preservation of Beers from the Wood predates the Campaign for Real Ale by a decade. It advocates the everyday use of wooden casks for the secondary fermentation – the cask-conditioning – and the dispensing of ordinary session-strength milds, bitters and stouts. Once you've got an oak firkin or two well broken in – once one or two old ales have passed through them – you could, if you wanted, forego completely polycasks and plastic pressure barrels and use wood instead. And lager tastes fine out of oak as well!

TIP 287: *Steam-clean your oak casks*

⬤ Sanitising oak casks used to be a nightmare – you would hear stories of brewery staff filling them with chains and then rolling them up and down the brewery yard, and all sorts of noxious chemicals being freely splashed about. No longer is this necessary. You can hire a steam pressure-cleaner instead, and if you put a bit of non-rinse cleaner into the reservoir, you'll have made your casks doubly clean! But if you're making sour beers, it's not always advisable to be too thorough – part of the charm of lambic is its unplanned and unknown blend of spores and bacilli (if you like that sort of thing). So, just the steam will do nicely.

TIP 288: *Fill casks with water for storage*

⬤ Casks are marvels of engineering, particularly when you consider that they were invented by the Gauls more than 2,000 years ago as a by-product of ship-building. They are simply (simple in theory, anyway) bevelled and chamfered staves, soaked or steamed for flexibility, hammered into a flanged base and then squeezed together by metal hoops. But if the staves are allowed to dry out they shrink, and you spring a leak. So when you're not using your oak cask fill it with water, with 5g ($^1/_5$oz) sodium metasulphite per litre for safety. To be doubly sure your casks are clean enough for use, you can always give them a big blast of CO_2 immediately before (outdoors, please!).

BOTTLING
AND KEGGING

Bottling is every brewer's least favourite task. The bottles are incredibly tricky to clean, the process is inevitably messy however careful you are, and it takes forever. But it's all worth it. Few things give the home brewer more pleasure than surveying a well-stocked cellar – other than emptying it, of course – and the beauty is that, having bottled, you don't need to polish off each brew before sampling the delights of the next.

BOTTLING

TIP 289: *Get collecting*

⬤ One of the ironies of home brewing – and this really is technically an irony – is that you need empty bottles more than anyone you know, but because you rarely buy beer you have fewer than anyone you know. You can, of course, buy bottles brand-new, but the most economical solution to your problem lies in the words 'anyone you know'. Tell all your neighbours, colleagues and relations to donate their empties if they want to stay friends. Ask them also to give the bottles a thorough swill as soon as they've used them to get rid of the stickiness microbes love. What's in it for them? One full bottle for every 20 empties? Okay, let's not get carried away – one full bottle every now and again.

TIP 290: *Soak your bottles*

⬤ No matter how well your expectant donors have rinsed out their offerings – and no matter how well you have rinsed out your own empties – they're still not clean enough. Every time an empty bottle comes your way, dunk it immediately in a tub of solvent that will get rid both of any remaining gunk and, hopefully, the label. In the last 25 years percarbonate-based stain removers such as OxiClean and PBW have become the standard chemical for achieving this, and very effective they are too. The strength of the solution should be 5mg per litre (2 pints) of water, and the bottles shouldn't be left for long in the solution or it will throw a chalky haze that can only be neutralised by an acid rinse.

TIP 291: Hold them down

⊕ Bottles will persist in floating, which means that only the submerged half of each one gets the benefit of the solvent. Putting the wire-mesh false bottom from your boiler and the slotted tube matrix from your mash tun on top of them will hold them down and ensure they all get a thorough inside-and-out soaking. It will also kill two birds with one stone by giving some of your brewing equipment an extra cleaning. If you need a bit of extra weight to hold the bottles down, your improvised bottle ice container (which is, of course, half-full of water) is ideal and can never have too much contact with sanitising solution.

TIP 292: Find a large enough vessel

⊕ Yes, it's true: you can't get fifty 0.5L (1 pint) beer bottles into a 25L (6½-gallon) brewing bucket. You can get the contents of the bucket into the bottles, but you can't get the bottles into the bin. And that's physics for you. You might, at the outset, have bought a 50L (13-gallon) catering bucket to convert into a boiler. Now that would be plenty big enough. If you didn't, go up in your loft and find your old baby bath, which is just ideal for the job.

TIP 293: *Use a bottle brush in addition to the solvent*

⬤ Bottle brushes used to be *de rigueur* but seem to have fallen out of favour. Partly that's because modern solvents seem to do the job perfectly well without their help, but it's also because, frankly, they aren't all that effective. They clean the sides of the bottle but not the bottom, and they might also transfer any lingering infection from a single bottle to the whole batch. By all means give the bottles a good brushing before they go into the solvent just to be on the safe side, but if you have a bottle with more sediment than the solvent alone will deal with you might be better off throwing it away.

TIP 294: *Sort and store your haul of bottles*

⬤ Once all visible gunk and tangible stickiness has gone, let your bottles dry and sort them by shape and size, because it's always nice to have each brew in the same kind of bottle. Throw out any that are chipped, scratched or scuffed; the minutest scratch is a luxury condo for bacteria and other microbes. You don't necessarily have to dump the clear glass ones, as was once recommended. Store them somewhere out of the way, in crates or boxes with lids to keep the spiders out. They're still not clean enough to use – for that they have to be sterile – but they're clean enough to store.

TIP 295: *The best bottles are beer bottles*

⬤ Or are they? Well yes, let's not be too precious about this, of course they are. But there's a caveat. Most brewery-packaged beer has been pasteurised, filtered and carbonated and is absolutely stable. The bottles, therefore, don't have to be any stronger than is necessary to withstand a predetermined pressure. You, on the other hand, are most likely going to bottle your beer live, with a low yeast count continuing to emit tiny puffs of CO_2. It'll probably never happen, but there is an outside chance that thin glass bottles will eventually blow their corks or even explode. When packaging stronger beers that you intend to lay down for any length of time, play it safe and go for a thicker bottle.

TIP 296: *Beware of "Champagne" bottles*

⬤ Just because a bottle is shaped like a Champagne bottle doesn't mean it is a Champagne bottle. A real Champagne bottle is ideal for the lengthy conditioning of both strong beers and beers that are meant to be especially spritzy, because frankly you could let off a hand grenade inside one and it would just narrow its eyes and light another cheroot. But many sparkling wines and fizzy cider and perry-style drinks are packaged in Champagne-shaped bottles to create a spurious image of quality. But if you use them, they will explode. Some of them have screw threads, which is a dead giveaway; others, though, will have mushroom corks just like the real thing. So check the weight: a sparkling wine bottle weighs about 400g (14oz) empty, like any other wine bottle; a modern Champagne bottle weighs 835g (30oz) and can withstand a pressure of 100psi.

TIP 297: *Reuse your Belgian beer bottles*

⚫ Many Belgian brewers use pressure bottles, some of which look just like Champagne bottles and some of which are straight-sided. The main difference is that Belgian bottles generally have narrower necks, so make sure you buy corks of the appropriate bore! There's another little caveat with Belgian bottles, too. Some home brewers use crown corks instead of mushrooms on pressure bottles, often with a wine cork driven in first, as a kind of belt and braces insurance policy. But the Belgian bottles with the rounded lip won't take a crown cap and will have to be properly corked and caged.

TIP 298: *Using swing-tops? Check their gaskets!*

⚫ Swing-tops are much prized by many home brewers, partly because they look so stylish, partly because they are so durable, and partly because they are the only bottles that don't need special capping equipment and are therefore easiest and quickest to fill. They have their drawbacks, though. One is that they're expensive to buy new, so whenever one crosses your path, don't throw it away! It's also sometimes said that the seals aren't always tight enough and that over time they can leak CO_2, leading to a dull and lifeless beer. In that case the gasket is at fault. Homebrew suppliers stock new ones, so change them regularly. And the same caveat applies as with Champagne bottles: some fancy-pants brands of soft drinks are sold in swing-top bottles that are too lightweight, and whose closures are too flimsy to be used by home brewers. Finally, the very sudden pressure release on opening can turn them into gushers or 'bottle bombs', so either fill them only with beers you reckon are already pretty stable, or open them occasionally during maturation to vent the excess gas.

TIP 299: *Avoid plastic*

⚫ PET is convenient in many ways. It's cheap, it's light, it can be efficiently sterilised, it's easy to fill and it's surprisingly robust. But – and this is a big but – it's gas-porous. In a surprisingly short time, maybe less than a month, it will allow the CO_2 to hiss gently away into the atmosphere, leaving the beer almost completely flat. PET and other plastic containers do have their place: if you don't bottle your beer but keep it in a cask or keg, you can draw off enough into a plastic bottle to take on your hike/to a friend's barbecue/to a bottle party. But that's it.

TIP 300: *There are no short-cuts in bottle washing*

⚫ Rigorous hygiene is vitally important at the bottling stage, not least because it would be a crying shame to nurse a whole brew through to the very last hurdle only to see it ruined by some stray infection. Your bottles must be as close to sterile as you can manage, as indeed must everything they come into contact with. All the taps, siphon tubes, funnels and bottle-tops must be as sterile as the bottles themselves, so bathe them all well in sodium metabisulphite immediately before use.

TIP 301: *Use the dishwasher*

⚫ Once you're ready to bottle, give your bottles a 20-minute bath in a 1–1.5% solution of household bleach or, better yet, a sodium metabisulphite solution of 10mg (or two crushed Campden tablets) per litre (2 pints) of hot water (sodium metabisulphite doesn't need rinsing). Whichever sanitiser you prefer, pop the bottles into the dishwasher without detergent or rinse aid but with the drying cycle turned on. That way they'll come out nice and clean and ready to use. It's important, though, to have freshly cleaned bottles, so this isn't a job you can do much in advance.

PRIMING

TIP 302: Time to wake up the beer

Having finished its primary fermentation and then had a nice long sleep, your beer might need to be woken up before bottling. Very experienced home brewers say there's no need to do this, but to be absolutely sure of getting a nice spritz into your bottles, you need to feed the surviving live yeast cells with a little sugar. Which type you decide to use will have an effect on the character of your beer. How much sugar you use is important, too: you want a light sparkle and a good head, not a bottle bomb!

TIP 303: Choose a sugar that complements your beer

You can use almost any sugar you choose to prime your beer with. One authority even suggests maple syrup, although one might draw the line at strawberry jam! For a lighter beer, or a beer whose flavour you don't want to alter, white sugar (preferably caster as it dissolves quicker) and corn syrup are pretty neutral. Dry malt extract will very slightly intensify your beer's character, especially extract of the same type of malt you brewed with. Honey will enrich a light beer and deepen a dark one; dark brown sugars, golden syrup and black treacle or molasses have strong flavours of their own which will come through, and are best kept for priming darker, stronger beers.

TIP 304: *Measure your priming sugar carefully*

❀ The idea of priming is to produce sufficient carbonation to give your beer a lift, and how much priming sugar you use will determine how much CO_2 there will be in your beer. British drinkers typically prefer their beer less carbonated than Americans and Australians. For an ordinary 25L (6$\frac{1}{2}$-gallon) brew 100g (3$\frac{1}{2}$oz) of white sugar, corn syrup, light brown sugar or invert sugar should produce a pressure of about 2.5 atmospheres. A British home brewer will probably use considerably less. Other sugars aren't 100% fermentable and you might need a touch more: 10% more DME or dark brown sugar; 20% more honey, golden syrup or molasses. You should keep fairly close to these measurements, especially with the more flavourful sugars. It may not look like a lot compared to the amount of beer it has to prime, but it will be enough. (The actual maths, in excruciating detail, is included in Chapter 8.)

TIP 305: *Make priming syrup with your own beer*

❀ Priming sugars should be made into a syrup before being added to the beer. This goes for liquid or semi-liquid additions such as corn syrup or honey as well as dry additions such as caster sugar (remember: cane, not beet!) or malt extract. The standard procedure is to dissolve the sugar in twice its own volume of boiling water and let it cool, although a twist is to use some of the beer you're about to add it to instead of water. It doesn't make a huge amount of difference, but it does mean you're not diluting the beer you've taken such pains over, and it is rather a nice flourish.

TIP 306: *Priming each bottle is soooo last year*

● It used to be customary to prime each bottle individually by hand, using a teaspoon. See the drawbacks? It takes forever; you risk distributing the priming syrup unevenly and getting a mixed batch of duds and bottle bombs; and since the average teaspoon is wider than the mouth of the average bottle you're bound to get sticky sweet sugar drips down the outside of the bottle – a 12-course banquet for bugs. It is much better to blend the priming syrup and the beer to be bottled in advance.

TIP 307: *Prime old, cold lager with extra yeast*

● A lager that's been slowly working away for 2 months or so – especially a strong one – is likely to need an extra shake if it's to have any spritz in the bottle. Prepare a single dose of the same strain of yeast you originally fermented it with and mix it with the priming syrup before you add them to the bottling bucket.

TIP 308: *Call up your Fourth Bucket!*

● We're not going to add the syrup to the beer in the pressure barrel because then we'd have to stir it, and at this stage we want to exclude oxygen as much as possible. So it's time for our old friend the Fourth Bucket to report for duty once again. Stand it on our other old friend, the sturdy step stool, and pour your priming syrup into it. Attach the siphon tube, with its end weighted by a piece of copper pipe as before, to the tap of the pressure barrel and transfer the primed beer slowly, with as little splashing and aeration as possible. The weighted end of the siphon tube should remain below the surface of the beer. When it's done, your Fourth Bucket has magically become your bottling bucket!

TIP 309: *Take Marvin Gaye and Kim Weston's advice*

⚫ Now is the time to gather together all your bottling equipment – starting with a friend because, as Marvin and Kim reminded us, it takes two. Well, it doesn't really, but this is a stage where (unless you're using swing-tops, in which case it doesn't make much difference) having a willing assistant/ long-suffering partner/wretched underling at the ready is really valuable. Because you have three options here: fill all 45-odd bottles and then cap them, which leaves them all standing around and open to infection for quite some time; fill and then cap each bottle, a repetitive task that will drive you mad by the 20th bottle; or fill each bottle and pass it to your accomplice to cap while you fill the next one. Well, which option would you choose?

TIP 310: *Sterilise your caps*

⚫ Your caps need to be as sterile as the bottles themselves, or all your efforts may be wasted. Douse them in a bowl of sanitiser for 20 minutes or so. The best chemical for this is one that doesn't need rinsing, so you (or your accomplice) can simply pick the caps out of the bowl of sanitiser as you need them. Sodium metabisulphite doesn't require rinsing since its active ingredient is SO_2 gas. There are also acid-based sanitisers such as Star San that don't need a rinse either.

TIP 311: *Drown corks in a Kilner jar*

⚫ If you thought floating bottles were hard to hold under water, wait until you try corks! There is one way, and one way only, to get wine corks thoroughly sterile, and that is to pack them as tight as you can into a Kilner jar (an old coffee jar will do fine, provided it's big enough) and then fill it right to the very brim with sanitiser before snapping/screwing the lid on.

TIP 312: *The more expensive cappers are easier to use*

⬤ Cappers come in two varieties: the two-handed and the one-handed bench capper. The two-handed is the cheaper since it doesn't have a stand of its own; you simply place the cap in the magnetised holder, put the capper on top of the bottle, squeeze the two handles down, and the job is done. The single-handed and much more expensive (although still not all that expensive) version has the advantage that you can hold the bottle firmly with one hand while operating the lever with the other. With the former option there is always the risk, by about bottle 30, of letting your attention wander and knocking the bottle over. With the latter there is no such danger.

TIP 313: *Capping pressure bottles*

⬤ There are four ways of capping pressure bottles, all of which are perfectly safe. The fancy way is to drive a proper cork about three-quarters of the way and fit a wire cage, winding its loop with a pencil or chopstick. The top end of the cork will compress into the proper mushroom shape under the pressure of the CO_2 given off by the beer. You may choose to buy a fancy corking lever for this operation, although an old-fashioned wooden flogger and mallet will do the job just as well. The second is to use a plastic mushroom and cage – adequate, but not very classy. The third (suitable only for Belgian bottles with straight necks... and for neurotic brewers!) is to cork it and then put a crown cap on as well. The fourth and simplest is simply to pop a crown cap on it; your supplier should have European (29mm) crown caps in stock if you're using real Champagne bottles.

TIP 314: *Don't fill bottles with a funnel*

⬤ Even with a run of 40-odd bottles, a straightforward pitcher and funnel would – you'd think – be the quickest and easiest method of filling. But that would not be bottling. That would be mere decanting, and is only an option for beer you intend to drink straight away. For, as with the transfer of beer from conditioning tank to bottling bucket, this is an operation where contact with air must be minimised. It's also advisable to lose as little beer as possible, not least because drips and spills are irresistible invitations to your microbial arch-enemies.

TIP 315: *Use a bottling stick*

⬤ The ingenious and inexpensive device that overcomes both of these problems is the bottling stick. This is simply a long tube with a one-way valve at the bottom. You just plug one end into the siphon tube (which you have already attached to the tap on your bottling bucket) and the other end into the bottle. It fills from the bottom, so no air; and while you're transferring it from one bottle to the next it shuts itself off, so no drips.

TIP 316: *Keep it dark*

⚫ Earlier we touched on the subject of clear-glass bottles and why their use might be avoided. It is commonly held that any beer stored in clear glass will inevitably be damaged by the condition known as 'lightstruck' – that is, the degradation of the isohumulones in the hop by ultraviolet light, which produces an off-flavour known as skunk or wet dog. Keep your bottles away from UV, though, and it won't happen. You might possess a stock of clear-glass bottles that you don't want to waste. You might just like the look of your beer in clear glass. In which case, keep it in a cardboard box in a place that is usually dark – for example, the garage – and only bring it out when you want to serve it. It'll be fine.

TIP 317: *Dress the bottles up nicely*

⚫ If you're proud of your beers, you'll want to share them, and if you want to share them (or even give them as gifts), you'll want them as handsomely dressed as possible. The labels themselves present few difficulties for anyone in possession of a computer and printer, although there is an argument between advocates of self-adhesive labels (easy to apply, harder to remove) and partisans of wet labels (messier to apply, easier to remove). The hard thing is to apply every label in precisely the same place on the bottle. Even the cheapest labelling machines are expensive, but with minimal woodworking skills you can make yourself a miniature cradle or sawhorse, the distance between the trusses being the same as the depth of the label. Lay your bottle in it and use the trusses as guides while you carefully apply the label. Job done. Complete the dressing with a heat-shrink capsule which looks nice and helps keep the spores and microbes at bay. Lovely!

KEGGING

TIP 318: *Keg your beer for longevity, freshness and sparkle*

⚫ Kegging your beer is, of course, a comparatively easy alternative to all the hassle of bottling it. But there's more to it than that. Not every drinker appreciates the comparatively low carbonation of British-style cask-conditioned beer, and not every brewer trusts an apparently unprotected beer to mature and then last without risking infection and oxidisation. By far the most common method of storing and dispensing draught beer around the world is to filter, pasteurise and carbonate it, after which it is completely sterile and will keep until Hell freezes over.

TIP 319: *Don't heed the naysayers!*

⚫ Kegging is decried by British beer-lovers who remember the 1960s and '70s, when the major brewers took the stability of processed beer as an excuse to reduce its alcohol content to the point where, in some cases, it was so weak that children could legally drink it! But this need not be the case. The keg method of storage and dispense won't harm a good beer any more than conditioning in a cask will improve a bad one. Discerning drinkers in Germany and Belgium are perfectly happy with it, and if it's good enough for them...

TIP 320: *Don't bother to pasteurise it*

● Mass-produced beers are commonly pasteurised to kill the last few surviving yeast cells, which, at this stage, are browsing on the remaining sugar but are no longer reproducing. This is a quality-control measure insofar as the brewer can be sure of despatching the beer into the uncertain world of retail with a precise and absolutely stable level of carbonation. It's hardly an issue for the home brewer; your beer is never going to leave the safety of your cellar for the labyrinthine world of haulage companies, wholesalers, off-licences and pubs. It has only a short journey to endure – from barrel to glass to mouth.

TIP 321: *You might even get away without filtering*

● If you've used Irish moss in the boil and fined thoroughly as described above, just run a little beer off from the secondary fermenter into a sight glass (or indeed any old glass, so long as it's clean) and satisfy yourself (a) that the beer is as clear as beer can be and (b) that all the sediment (brewing jargon for dead yeast and other bits and pieces) must therefore be lying below the level of the outflow. Then connect your hose or siphon tube to the tap of your fermenter and run it slowly into your keg to minimise turbulence, using your bottling stick to avoid contact with oxygen. If, when you come to drink it, the beer doesn't pour absolutely 100% clear, inform your guests that the haze is perfectly natural (as it is) and is a good source of Vitamin B.

TIP 322: *Filtration is generally best*

● Keg dispense works by pumping CO_2 into the barrel to force the beer out under pressure. This necessarily creates a fair bit of turbulence, raising the sediment from its resting place at the bottom of the keg into an unappealing cloudy suspension. And after all your hard work you don't want to run the risk of having to make excuses, do you? So, filtration it is.

TIP 323: *Treat and chill your beer first*

● This is your last chance to get rid of any stubborn proteins that, if not removed, might choke the filter cartridge and will certainly cause chill haze in your beer. Two or three days before filtration treat the beer with additional finings and a clarifying agent such as silica gel, then, using your immersion cooler and ice bottles as necessary, get it down as close to freezing as you can. Chilling the beer will also make carbonating it easier. Try to get your filtration vessels and keg as cold as possible, too.

TIP 324: *Lay out all your kit*

● Filtration always seems like a fiendishly complicated affair – as fiendishly complicated, indeed, as assembling a flat-pack wardrobe. But like all these things, it becomes a little less intimidating once you have grasped the principle and laid out all the kit. The principle is simple: in a closed system, the beer is forced under CO_2 through a filter from one tank to another, scrubbing out not only the last few solid particles but also almost all the oxygen. The kit's not all that complicated either: two Cornelius kegs, a bottle of gas and a filter unit with all its various connectors and bits of hose. Oh, and of course a brewing bucket to stand the filter unit in (it's going to spurt!).

TIP 325: *Sterilise everything*

⚫ Essentially what you're doing when you filter and keg your beer is creating a closed system. Every last molecule you put in there is going to stay in there, to wreak what havoc it can (although not much ought to be able to survive all the CO_2 you're going to be spraying about the place. You might not survive it yourself if you don't open a window!). Fill a bucket (yes, another one) with your sodium metabisulphite solution and give absolutely everything a good long bath: filter unit, connectors, hoses, the lot. Wash down all exterior surfaces including the gas bottle with your bleach wipes.

TIP 326: *Choose a filter size*

⚫ Big industrial brewers commonly push their keg beers through a filter with one-micron pores – or even in some cases 0.45-micron pores – to ensure absolute clarity. Now a micron is one-thousandth of a millimetre, and there aren't many clumps of protein that can squeeze through it. A home brewer, though, might well object that some of the solids remaining in the beer are actually flavour components, and while filtering them all out might ensure dazzling clarity, it also reduces the character of the beer. A 5-micron filter is therefore more common among home brewers.

TIP 327: *Flush the air out of your Cornies*

⚫ The first stage in filtration is to connect the gas bottle to the first of your Cornelius kegs and give it a 20-second squirt of CO_2 at about 5psi to flush out all the air. Put the lid back on and give it a blast at 20psi, bleed the outlet valve in the lid, and repeat two or three times. Then do the same with your second Cornie. The filter can be connected to the second keg while it's being flushed to ensure that it, too, gets its dose of CO_2, ensuring the sudden death of almost any stray microbes.

TIP 328: *Connect everything and blast away!*

● Now it's time to connect the two kegs via the filter and run your beer off from your conditioning or lagering vessel into the first keg. Turn up the gas to 20psi and just let it rip. You will have observed that your filtration unit is transparent. This is so that you can ensure it's absolutely full throughout the process. If it's not, press the purge button until you get the little spurt of escaping beer (see? I told you it was going to spurt!) that tells you the filter is as full as it can be. It should take no more than 10 minutes at most to fill the second keg, at which point, disconnect everything and clean it thoroughly.

TIP 329: *Now pressurise the beer*

● This is the last step in kegging. The beer in the dispense keg needs to be saturated with CO_2 both as a preservative and to create the pressure necessary for dispense. There are two ways of doing this: the slow way and the quick way. The slow way is to hook the keg up to the gas bottle and carbonate at 30psi for 3 days. The quick way is to hook up the keg and the bottle, blast until the hissing stops, turn off the gas and give the keg a really good shaking. Repeat until there is no more hissing to be heard; at this point the beer can be considered well and truly carbonated. If you've succeeded, you should need a dispense pressure of no more than 5psi and hopefully rather less.

CONTROL AND TROUBLESHOOTING

Good beer is the successful end product of a myriad of variables, including ingredients, quantities, temperatures, times, routines and conditions. All of these need to be kept under control. Things can and will go wrong, though, and it's important to know what to do to put it right. The following is largely a recap and expansion on tips you'll already have come across, all gathered together for ease of reference because prevention is always better than cure!

RECORD KEEPING

TIP 330: *Keep a brewing book*

🔘 No matter how good your memory is, you will soon lose track of what you've brewed, when, how and, indeed, how it turned out! Record keeping that is both compendious and assiduous is the only way to be certain of what your next brew will be like. Before long, your brewer's book will become the most important piece of kit in your collection, enabling you to recreate with confidence a beer you might not have brewed for years. It will need to be a big book. And it will need a wipe-down cover!

TIP 331: *Keep records as you go*

🔘 However tired you are, however pressing your next engagement may be, set down in your brewer's book whatever you've just done the very moment you have finished doing it – or even while you're doing it, if you have your hands free for a moment. The whole point of the brewer's book is precision and although you might just still remember every detail when you get back from the shops or have finished your cup of tea or have had a good night's sleep, there's no guaranteeing it. In brewing, as in life, there is no more propitious moment than right now!

TIP 332: *Every beer tells a story*

⚫ Every beer you brew should have a page to itself, and each page must tell the entire story of the beer, starting with what kind of beer it is and detailing the malt grist, the date you mashed it in, the volume and the gravity at the end of mashing. Next, note the hop varieties and weights, and the points during the boil when you made the additions. Note the wort cooling procedures and timing. All the above is an entirely objective record of actualities: the length and volatility of primary fermentation; the date racked to secondary fermentation; the length of the secondary fermentation. Your assessment of the primary fermentation will be to a certain extent subjective, but as long as you develop a vocabulary and stick to it that's fine. The important thing is that your records will allow you to discover where – or if, that is – you went wrong, to correct errors, and to replicate every beer in the book. It's also useful to give each beer a batch or gyle number to cross-reference with the label.

TIP 333: *Include tasting notes*

⚫ Now this bit really is subjective. But if you've followed the training procedures set out in Chapter 1, you should be able to conclude each beer's record with a full set of tasting notes: appearance, aroma, palate, mouthfeel and finish. This is important because the proof of the beer is in the drinking and if you have made a mistake somewhere along the line, this is when you're going to find out about it. Certainly, at the beginning of your brewing career you might want help with this – gather a small tasting party to assess each brew and make sure it includes women, whose sense memory is proven to be more accurate than men's. In time you'll have the experience to taste all by yourself but at first – hey, let's party!

TIP 334: *Beer tasting shouldn't be too much fun!*

🌐 Informal beer-tasting sessions, in which people can express themselves in terms that tend to grow wilder and more far-fetched as the session goes on, are a lot of fun. Your tasting sessions are a bit more serious. You're trying to match the results of your brewing against what you expected from the ingredients and processes, and the notes you come up with are a serious reference work to aid you in future brews. So be sober, be rigorous and above all be consistent in the way you describe and record different characteristics.

TIP 335: *Remember to look after your tasting glasses*

🌐 Use clean glasses for tasting sessions. Rinse them thoroughly with very hot water after washing, and allow them to dry naturally on a wire rack so that no bad odours form inside. Dirty glassware leads to collapsed beer foam and taints. Use small stemmed glasses and don't overfill; you want room enough in the glass to swirl and sniff!

TIP 336: *Include useful information on the label*

⚫ Although you'll want your bottled beer to look good, the label should also act as an *aide-mémoire* to tell you something about what you're drinking. So include the bottling date at the very least and perhaps also a brief summary of the malt and hop grists and the yeast. Also include the gyle number, if you're using them. If something's wrong (or right!) with the beer, it's easier and quicker to look it up using a gyle number.

TIP 337: *Use the flavour wheel!*

⚫ The American Society of Brewing Chemists came up with the flavour wheel to help define and describe flavours and odours. Here's a simplified version of it for you.

HYGIENE

TIP 338: Take hygiene to heart

⚫ You've been lectured so often in this book about the importance of absolute hygiene that you're probably thoroughly fed up with it. But it is something that really has to become second nature. Brewing is such an involved and intricate process that it would be worse than a shame to lose a brew to a stray spore, and beer is such a fragile creature that it can happen very easily. It's not a question of being neurotic or obsessive; it's a question of developing good habits. In due course, you shouldn't even notice that you're constantly cleaning your hands with antibacterial gel and running a bleach wipe over the last thing you touched.

TIP 339: Hygiene is even more important to the brewer than it is to the cook!

⚫ Few kitchens are surgically clean, and if yours is, you run a greater risk of getting sick because you have no chance to build up immunities. Hospital staff rarely contract hospital-acquired illnesses because they're constantly exposed to low-level doses of the pathogens concerned. Patients do, because they're suddenly exposed to lethal doses. Think of your beer as a hospital patient: it will never acquire an immunity to the kind of infections your own body shrugs off with devil-may-care *sangfroid*.

TIP 340: *Good hygiene is a two-phase operation*

⬤ Hygiene consists of two separate but necessary and complementary operations: cleaning and sterilising. You clean everything after you've used it to remove any solids or residues that might harbour bacteria and other unwanted life forms. You sterilise everything before you use it again to get rid of any bacteria that might have survived the cleaning or crept back in after it. In between times, you store everything under wraps and away – as far as possible – from the ordinary traffic of everyday life.

TIP 341: *Clean before you sterilise*

⬤ Cleaning is not the same as sterilising. Cleaning is simply keeping the ground clear so there's nowhere for colonies of bacteria and spores to shelter and grow. In short, thorough cleaning is not good hygiene but makes good hygiene possible.

TIP 342: *Follow the procedure*

⬤ Which basically is as follows: soak in detergent; brush out; rinse thoroughly; soak for 20 minutes in sterilant; rinse thoroughly again; dry; put away. Do that, and when the next brewing day rolls around you'll already be more than halfway to the level of sterility you need.

TIP 343: *Try stain remover in the first wash*

⊙ Soaking everything in a stain remover such as OxiClean is already recommended for bottles and won't do the rest of your equipment any harm. The advantage of stain remover is that it will effectively dissolve grease and glue that an ordinary household detergent won't touch. One alternative is an environmentally friendly alkaline-based detergent such as powdered brewer's wash (PBW) at about 25g per litre (2 pints) of water. A good 20-minute soak in warm water will soften and loosen most residues and other solids.

TIP 344: *Clean with soft brushes*

⊙ A long soak is all very well, but some of the more awkward items – especially any screw threads and sharp elbows in pipework – could do with a good brushing out too, just to be sure. But if there's one place a couple of newly wed bacteria would absolutely love to move in to, to call home, to raise a family in, it's a scratch. So do your cleaning with plastic brushes and scourers, not metal ones. Old toothbrushes, softened by use, are too valuable ever to throw away; they will get into corners and angles that scourers and bigger brushes can't reach. A caution, though: bacteria aren't fussy about where they live and will happily colonise your brushes and scourers, so make sure these are sterile or you'll be importing more trouble than you're getting rid of!

TIP 345: *Rinse with determination*

⬤ The purpose of the first wash is to loosen and lift solids, which we have now done. An energetic sluicing under fast-running water, rather than a mere jiggling about in a washing-up bowl of tepid gunk, is mandatory to carry away all the solids that have been thus loosened and lifted. Inner surfaces of larger vessels need to be rinsed with equal vim and vigour. Don't just wipe them over with a damp rag (damp rags DO NOT belong in breweries!); get them under that tap, turn it on full and swill and empty multiple times.

TIP 346: *Pick a chemical, any chemical*

⬤ Now that all the hidey-holes where pathogens might take shelter have been sluiced away, the next step is to sterilise/sanitise, wiping out any surviving pathogens and creating a harsh environment that will deter them from growing back. But what to use? The fact is that there are dozens of sterilants out there, some proprietary, some not, and some even formulated with the home brewer in mind. After trying various options, you'll quickly get an idea of which you prefer. But for now, why not start with good old-fashioned bleach?

TIP 347: *How strong is your bleach?*

● Sodium hypochlorite is the chemical that gives bleach most of its strength, but the sodium hypochlorite content of different brands varies enormously, from as little as 1.1% to as much as 5%. The home brewer's standard 1.5% bleach solution can therefore be so weak as to be virtually ineffective. Always choose a brand that declares its sodium hypochlorite percentage and go for the stronger end of the scale. Try to avoid heavily perfumed brands, although this can be removed by vigorous rinsing.

TIP 348: *Caustic soda makes it more effective still*

● Most of what you have to clean off your brewing equipment will be the organic residues of the brewing process itself: proteins, fats, yeast residue and carbohydrates. The effectiveness of your bleach solution in tackling these residues will be considerably boosted by the addition of a pinch of caustic soda (sodium hydroxide), which is alkaline (some brands of bleach already contain it – check the label). But caustic soda is awesome stuff, so rinse extra-well if you're using it.

TIP 349: *Bleach is not the only sterilant*

● Many home brewers don't like bleach. They don't trust it and think it causes off-flavours. They prefer an acid-based sterilant, generally a very dilute phosphoric acid available as proprietary brands such as Star San. Star San claims to be effective after a contact of two minutes with a solution of just a gram per litre (2 pints) of water, and it certainly has its supporters. Unlike alkalines, it's also effective against mineral deposits such as limescale and beerstone (calcium oxalate), so if you're in a hard water area it will protect your equipment and deprive pathogens of places to hide.

TIP 350: *An important safety notice*

● DO NOT mix acid-based products with bleach. The two combined produce chlorine gas which, if it doesn't actually kill you, will certainly do you no good! Learn from the pain suffered by a fool who tried to unblock a bath with neat bleach and, when that didn't work, poured a powerful proprietary acid-based unblocker down after it. The bathroom filled immediately with dense and stinging white gas in a potentially lethal concentration. Ouch!

TIP 351: *Now rinse and dry*

● Acid-based sterilants don't need rinsing because they break down by themselves. Alkaline sterilants most definitely do, though, especially those with caustic soda in them! The dishwasher is the best place for rinsing anything that'll fit into it (no rinse aid, remember!) because it will dry them too, and if there's one thing a bacterium loathes it's anywhere that's hot and dry. Give the bigger vessels a good rinse too.

TIP 352: *Safe storage will aid good hygiene*

● Whether in use or in store, vessels and accessories all need to be well protected from contamination. Piling everything up in the garden shed or a corner of the garage is an open invitation to contaminants of all sorts. So fix two things: a clean and dry storage environment without too much in the way of cobwebs, plaster dust, etc, preferably somewhere that can be swept, dusted and vacuumed before use; and bags and boxes to put everything in.

TIP 353: *Keep bits and pieces you use often in a sterilant bath*

⚫ Once cleaned, rinsed and dried, smaller equipment, such as hydrometers, thermometers, airlocks, siphon tubes, sieves, brushes and measuring spoons, can be stored in a 25L (6½-gallon) brewing bucket with a tight snap-on lid. If you brew regularly, you can provide extra protection by keeping it in a couple of litres of 5% sodium metabisulphite solution. Sodium metabisulphite works, as you know, by releasing SO_2 gas, which will fill the headspace of your bucket and keep up the silent war on microbes while you sleep. If you're an infrequent brewer, though, it's better to dry it after cleaning and keep it that way.

TIP 354: *You've cleaned... now sterilise!*

⚫ It's brewing day. You've assembled all the vessels and accessories you're going to use and, because you cleaned them thoroughly and effectively before you put them away last time, they won't be difficult to render microbiologically virginal. Forget about the boiler – it'll sterilise itself! – but all other vessels should be wiped down either with the standard 5% sodium metabisulphite solution or 1.5% bleach solution. If using the latter, rinse everything well after sterilising. Accessories, especially taps, should be dunked in a sodium metabisulphite bath for 20 minutes.

TIP 355: *Make friends with peracetic acid*

⚫ Peracetic acid is a compound of peroxide and acetic acid, widely used as a sterilant not just in food and drink manufacture but also in air-conditioning units, where it effectively kills the *legionella* virus. It works by oxidising the outer membranes of pathogenic microorganisms, including bacteria and spores, so it's pretty useful stuff for the home brewer. Better yet, it's non-rinse and can be purchased as a spray. So, for added insurance, give everything you've just sterilised and rinsed a good puff of peracetic acid immediately before use.

TIP 356: *Don't forget the surfaces*

⚫ It's not just your brewing equipment that needs to be clean. All the kitchen surfaces you'll be using need to be thoroughly cleaned and disinfected before you get busy. And while you're at it you might as well clean the rest of the kitchen too: best to be sure, and it's an opportunity to placate the rest of the family. Oh, and strictly no pets allowed in on brewing day!

TIP 357: *Now wash your hands!*

⚫ Now you've cleaned and disinfected everything you can, the biggest potential source of contamination here is you! So don't try brewing in your gardening clothes, and have frequent recourse to a hospital-grade antibacterial gel dispenser (preferably one that actually contains some hospital-grade antibacterial gel!).

PROCESS CONTROL

TIP 358: *Check and record the quality of your raw materials*

⬤ It's good to get into the habit of checking your ingredients. OK so you don't have a lab, but you do have some quite sensitive gear to hand: your eyes, nose, and mouth! A magnifying glass is useful to help assess the crushed malt prior to mashing (you're looking for long sections of husk that are well cracked). Pop some in your mouth; if it's a bit crunchy it could be poorly modified.

MATERIAL	FREQUENCY	METHOD
Malt	Every brew	Taste, odour, appearance, evenly crushed?
Hops	Every brew	Appearance, odour (rub and sniff), appearance, taste (make a tea)
Water	Every brew	Taste, odour, pH
Yeast	Every brew	If using wet yeast then: odour, appearance
Mash	Every brew	pH, temperature, saccharification (iodine test)
Wort collection	Every brew	Taste, odour, clarity, pH, gravity of the first and last runnings
Collected wort to FV	Every brew	Colour, pH, taste, odour, clarity
Wort in FV	Every day	OG, pH, temperature
Finished beer at racking	Every brew	FG, pH, taste, odour, clarity

TIP 359: *Watch your weight*

● Quantities are crucial in brewing, and while you might weigh out your malt in kilograms or pounds, you're measuring out your hops and some adjuncts such as Irish moss in grams and ounces. If you're in any doubt at all about the accuracy of your kitchen scales, invest in a digital set to make doubly sure you weigh out the smaller quantities accurately.

TIP 360: *When to take the temperature*

● Temperature control is important at so many different stages of the brewing process. Take the temperature at all stages and remember to record it. Temperature variations of even 2°C (3°F) can influence the outcome. Where possible, try to correct as necessary by adding a little hot or cold water as appropriate.

TIP 361: *When to check pH*

● It's the same with the acidity. Check it throughout, using pH test papers or a pH meter. It is possible to make slight corrections by adding acid but harder to take acidity away. If anything appears excessive, for example, a mash pH of 7 or a beer pH of 2, then it should be investigated. Here are some guidelines on target pH levels (all as measured at 20°C [68°F]):

• Hot liquor: 6.2–6.5 (ales) 6.7–7 (lagers)
• Mash: 5.3–5.6
• Wort (pre-boil): 5.4–5.7
• Wort (post-boil): 5.2–5.5
• Beer: 3.9–4.2 (ale) and 4.2–4.5 (lager)

TIP 362: *Learn when to check the gravity*

⚙ Take gravity readings with your hydrometer or refractometer at all key stages: first wort runnings, last wort runnings, pre-boil, post-boil and throughout the fermentation. Remember, you can correct certain variations by dilution (liquoring back) or adding additional sugar. It will probably take at least three brews of each of your beers to fine-tune the recipe and procedure, but patience pays off and you ought to get a consistent brew every time after that.

TIP 363: *Learn when to check clarity*

⚙ Check the clarity of your runnings from the mash tun and don't forget to 'vorlauf', which will help remove some of the larger particles. It's also good practice to record the clarity post-boil by letting a small tumbler of wort cool down from boiling to ambient. This will show you the different levels of 'break' and see if the boil was effective. Don't worry if your wort is slightly hazy pre-boil or has a touch of dullness going into the fermenter. This should all sort itself out. However, if you've got a pea soup it would be cause for concern!

TROUBLESHOOTING

TIP 364: *When mash conversion is poor*

 You've done an iodine test and it's clear (ie, yellow), but the level of extract seems poor. So what's gone wrong? Occasionally this will be down to incorrect milling of the grist, which leads to your particle size being too coarse or too fine. If you've bought pre-ground malt that shouldn't be the problem, whereas it might be if you're grinding it yourself. More likely causes are: you didn't mash-in evenly and you've got dry lumps; the pH is wrong, which means the enzymes aren't working at their best; or the temperature of the mash is outside the 62–67°C (144–153°F) range. Go back and check your notes to see if one of these is possible. If it's something obvious – the temperature or pH is wrong, say – adjust it next time. Remember, you can adjust low extract by the addition of sugar or DME. Is your kit doing the job? Some small mash tuns can lose a lot of heat and may well need extra insulation. Are your thermometer and pH strips (or meter) accurate? Did you remember to add the calcium salts or are they still sitting on the sideboard in a little dish? Ooops! It happens.

TIP 365: Has the wort run-off slowed to a trickle?

⚙ When the wort just won't flow from the mash tun, the most obvious cause is that the mash bed has settled on the tube matrix and clogged up the outlets. This shouldn't happen if you're using a finely drilled false bottom that will support the weight of the grain bed. Turn everything off and refloat the mash bed by running in a little hot water (recording volume and temperature in your brewing book), giving it a gentle stir with your paddle, allowing everything to calm down a bit, and then starting the run-off again. Another cause might be the high levels of beta-glucans in your cereal adjuncts, which thicken the wort. Again, a little water is the immediate answer.

TIP 366: Or does the wort gush too fast?

⚙ You're sparging all wrong! The sparge water absolutely must be gently and evenly distributed: too much, too fast, on one spot will create a channel through the mash bed which the wort will simply flood through. If sparging by hand, be more gentle; if you're using a sparging arm, reset it.

TIP 367: Fix problems after the boil is over

⚙ The best time to correct any deficiencies that have appeared in the mash tun is after the boil, in the wort cooler. If acidity turns out to have been the problem, adjust it now using gypsum to increase it or chalk to lower it. If the problem was either temperature or a blocked filter and you had to add water, your gravity will have fallen; use corn or invert sugar (not beet sugar, which causes off-flavours) to get it back up. In a 25L (6½-gallon) brew every 100g (3½oz) of sugar will raise the gravity by 1.54. So, take a hydrometer reading; if, for example, you need a gravity of 1057og and your wort is at 1054, you need to add 230g (8¹/₁₀oz) of sugar. Dilute it slightly with some wort, mix it well and add either to the wort cooler or the FV.

TIP 368: *Dealing with stuck fermentation: poor aeration*

⬤ Sometimes that terrible moment comes when you've pitched your yeast and you're waiting for it all to happen – and it doesn't. No dense rocky head, or not much of one. Scarcely a bubble eructates from the pristine surface of your wort. A day crawls by. By the time you're halfway through the second day you know you've got a stuck ferment. If it's still early days, what's probably happened is that you haven't been aerating sufficiently along the way, and however lovestruck all the little yeasts are they can't reproduce because they haven't got enough to breathe, poor wee darlings. But don't despair! You can help! Just grab a bucket, run off a couple of litres (½ gallon) of wort, and then pour it back into the fermenter from a great height, with as much splashing as you can manage. Repeat this a few times. Then grab your paddle and give a few minutes' mighty stirring, replace the lid and wait for the reproducing to commence!

TIP 369: *Dealing with stuck fermentation: yeast malnutrition*

⬤ Okay, so it wasn't poor aeration. That's not the only cause of a stuck ferment, but as it's the easiest to treat that's what we tried first. Here's another. In days of yore, or so it's said, when cidermakers found their vats had stopped bubbling they'd chuck in a dead rat. Your stuck ferment could well be down to yeast malnutrition, especially if the recipe included high levels of sugar and other adjuncts, and a chunk of decomposing meat will produce enough nitrogen to get the yeast going again. Although a bit of bacon would probably work better than a rat, neither is what you really want in your beer. An additional dose of yeast nutrient, used according to the instructions on the packet and followed by a cautious stir, would probably work better than either of them.

TIP 370: Dealing with stuck fermentation: insufficient yeast

● Fermentation can also stick if you've pitched with insufficient yeast or if the yeast you've used is just too unwell or too old for all that heavy breathing and furious reproduction. The answer here is simple: make up another starter and whack it in, making sure this time that the yeast isn't past its expiration date, and didn't come in a split or otherwise damaged packet (which might have allowed it to become spoiled or infected). Once you've pitched your new yeast, aerate the wort and give it a really good stir.

TIP 371: Stir your yeast if it overflocculates

● No, that isn't really a word, but some strains do have a tendency to clump together and drift to the bottom of the fermenter where they do nobody any good at all. This is easier to detect if you're using a glass or plastic carboy than an opaque brewing bucket as your secondary fermenter, but a gentle and deep stir (also known as rousing) – going right to the bottom of the fermenter – carried out at the same time every day should be enough to persuade the yeast not to be so damned lazy.

TIP 372: A chiller is also a warmer

⊛ Sometimes the temperature is just wrong – either you pitched at the wrong temperature (you should aim for 18–20°C [64–68°F] for ale, 10–12°C [50–54°F] for lager), or you pitched at the right temperature but the wort has subsequently warmed up or cooled down. Ale yeasts in particular don't like the cold – they curl up and fall into a deep sleep at anything less than 14°C (57°F). If that's the case, just reach for your immersion coil and instead of passing cold water through it – you've guessed! – pass hot water though it, keeping a close eye on that thermometer. Then check your insulation to make sure it can maintain the optimum temperature (66°C [151°F] for ale) for as long as need be. As with the lazy flocculators above, give ale worts that have been overchilled a deep, gentle stir after warming them up.

TIP 373: Your beer's cloudy? Fine!

⊛ Unless the haze is caused by bacterial or other infection it won't affect the taste. If, on the other hand, it is caused by an infection – well, you certainly won't want to drink it! But all home brewers like their beer to look its best and are disappointed with a hazy batch. And this is a case where prevention is definitely easier than cure! The only answer to cloudy beer is to fine in the cask or bottling bucket either with isinglass, silicone gel or polyvinylpolypyrrolidone.

TIP 374: *Do a cask finings test*

● If you're going to use isinglass for cask fining then it's a good idea to undertake what's known as a finings test. It's simple enough but will, unfortunately, use up a bit of your precious brew. But not to worry, because once you've done it a couple of times, and provided you do everything consistently, it shouldn't need to be done more than once every six or seven brews of that particular beer to make sure everything is on track. So how to do a finings test? This is the basic set-up required for a cask finings test. Dose three 250ml (½-pint) glasses of your beer with 1g, 2g and 3g of isinglass and leave to stand for an hour at 15–18°C (59–65°F).

A   B   C

Then simply multiply the dose by the amount of beer you wish to fine and add it to the cask when you fill it. Looking at the examples above you can see that sample A has insufficient finings, so there's a small compact bottom layer of yeast but the layer above has not dropped properly and could take longer to drop bright in the cellar or even not clear completely. Sample B has dropped a good solid compact bottom without much 'fluffiness' above it and a relatively clear liquid. It is therefore the right dose to use. Sample C has dropped a compact bottom, as in Sample B, but has a layer of excess fluffy finings above it containing some large flocs, in which case too much has been added.

TIP 375: *You have a fluffy bottom*

● Sometimes it's possible to add a little too much isinglass to cask ale, which results in a fluffy bottom on the cask floor. Isinglass needs yeast cells to form the flocs that drop out of suspension; insufficient yeast means no flocs. Therefore the excess cask finings sit in a murky cloud just by the tap outlet. The solution? Do a finings test and add only enough or even just under the required dose of isinglass.

TIP 376: *Your cask beer starts off clear but then turns cloudy over a couple of days*

● This is usually a sign that you've got a bacterial or wild yeast infection. Not much you can do except drink it, provided it still smells and tastes okay. If you leave it, you will most likely start to detect sour milk, vinegary, or spicy clovelike notes, which will confirm that the little blighters are the culprits. Answer? Tighten up on hygiene!

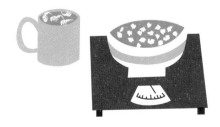

TIP 377: *Inefficient cask fining action*

⚫ You're convinced everything has been done properly but you still have hazy beer. There are a number of reasons for the finings not working or working too slowly:

- Yeast count too high – Do cask finings test prior to dosing.
- Finings have degraded in storage – Isinglass should be stored at 5–10°C (41–50°F) and used within 4–6 weeks of purchase. Don't buy more than you need!
- Incorrect pH – Beer pH should be 3.8–4.2 (ale). The cask finings performance is impaired below pH 3.5. Check the beer pH.
- Wild yeast contamination – Wild yeast doesn't interact with isinglass in the same manner as brewing yeast. Check for off-taints to confirm.
- Starch in beer – Check for starch presence with an iodine test. If present, look at your mashing regime as being a possible cause of the problem.

TIP 378: *Lack of condition in bottle or cask*

⚫ We all like a good head and a bit of life in our glass. However, very occasionally you can appear to have a beer which lacks life, or carbonation, when poured. So what's the problem? It's usually down to one of two things and here they are with their solutions:

- Too little residual sugar left over from primary fermentation – Add primings when racking off to give the yeast something to munch on to produce that all-important CO_2 fizz.
- Insufficient yeast count at time of bottling – Not enough yeast left in the beer at time of bottling, so check your yeast dosing and increase it slightly.

TIP 379: *Calculate the quantity of priming sugar you need with precision*

● The amount of CO_2 in beer is measured in 'volumes': one volume is equal to 1.96g of CO_2 per litre (2 pints). Cask ale might have 1 or 1.5 volumes when pulled through a handpump; keg and bottle beers can have as much as 3.5–5 volumes. Most people would expect to use 1tsp of sugar per litre of beer to generate the fizz they want. But if you want to be exact, here's the maths. The factors to consider are:

A The volume of beer you are bottling (note: this includes the water in which you dissolve your priming sugar).

B The amount of CO_2 produced by a gram of sugar (0.46g, in fact).

C The amount of CO_2 already in the beer before adding the primings – a difficult one because we can't measure it as such. In general, 1.5 volumes (2.94g CO_2/L) is a good guess.

D The amount of CO_2 you want to end up with in the bottle – anywhere between 2–5 volumes (3.92–9.8g CO_2/L), depending on the style of beer.

So to calculate the required CO_2 you want to add to the bottle (E), it's simply: D – C = E. Let's say your beer contains our estimated 1.5 volumes or 2.94g of CO_2/L and you want 3 volumes or 5.88g/L in total, then your difference is 1.5 volumes (2.94g/L) of CO_2.

For your whole bottling run the amount of sugar to be added is: (A x E) / B. In all probability you've ended up with around 23L (6 gallons) of beer for bottling plus 0.25L (½ pint) of water for dissolving the sugar, giving a total of 23.25L. This is the amount by which you need to multiply the additional CO_2 you want, which in this case is 2.94g/L. This is then divided by 0.46 to give you the amount of sugar to add in total. So we would have: (23.25 x 2.94) / 0.46 = 148.6g of sugar.

TIP 380: *How much yeast is required to condition bottled beer?*

⦿ In general a yeast count of a million cells per millilitre is needed for successful bottle conditioning, and maybe double that for high-strength beers with a gravity of 1075og or more. Commercial brewers will use a haemocytometer and microscope to make a cell count – something to put on your wish list! The easiest method for everyone else is to fine the beer to be bottled with isinglass in the FV to get the primary fermentation yeast count down as low as possible. Wait at least 8 hours for the finings to do their job before transferring the beer to your bottling bucket or container, using a siphon to exclude air. Slowly stir in the measured dose of primings, trying not to admit any air. You now need to add your dried bottling yeast.

TIP 381: *There are special yeast strains for conditioning in the bottle*

⦿ Choose a good-quality bottling yeast whose flocculation pattern needs to be medium-high to give a solid compact bottom in the bottle. A gram (⅛oz) of dried yeast will create around 20,000,000,000 yeast cells. In other words, a lot! So for a beer that had gravity of over 1075og you might wish to add around 3.5g of bottling yeast to your 23.5L (6 gallons) of beer but perhaps only half that amount, 1.75g, for a beer of 1030–1075og. Rehydrate the bottling yeast as per normal rehydration instructions, wait as usual, and then add to the beer to be racked off and stir it in gently. Now bottle!

TIP 382: *Let it condition!*

⦿ Once bottled, it's best to let the beer condition in a warm place for at least a week if not two, aiming for a temperature of 17–20°C (63–68°F). Then just pop the bottles into your usual cold storage area at 10–12°C (50–54°F) for another week and it should be ready to enjoy.

DETECTING AND AVOIDING OFF-FLAVOURS

TIP 383: *Some common fermentation and yeast-derived flavours and aromas*

⬤ Learning some of the more common flavours and aromas we find in finished beer can be a huge help in identifying any possible fault, thus narrowing down where it might have come from, or perhaps defining a particular beer style. Here's a list of the most common ones:

Alcoholic	Ethyl alcohol (think neat vodka)
Green apples/emulsion paint	Acetaldehyde
Solvent-like, fruity, pear drops	Ethyl, iso-butyl, amyl, beta-phenyl acetates
Phenolic: Clovelike/Herbal	4-Vinyl and ethyl guaiacol
Medicinal (TCP/sticking plaster)	Various chlorophenols
Smoky	Guaiacol (flavour), syringol (aroma)
Fatty acid (cheesy)	Valeric acid
Buttery/butterscotch	Diacetyl
Rancid	Caproic acid
Cooked vegetable/sweetcorn	Dimethyl sulphide (DMS)
Cardboard/papery	Trans-2-Nonenal
Acetic/sharp/vinegary	Acetic acid
Sour	Lactic acid
Sweetness	Sugar (Glucose, fructose, maltose, chloride)
Bitterness	Iso-alpha-acid, melanoidins (roast malt colour)
Metallic/bloodlike	Iron, copper, zinc
Carbonation/bubbles	Carbon dioxide

It's important to remember that not all of these are undesirable and some, in moderation, can enhance the character of a beer.

TIP 384: *Identify smells of green apples or emulsion paint*

⚫ Chances are you're smelling acetaldehyde. This compound appears at two points in the normal beer cycle, once during fermentation when the beer is young and again when the beer has been exposed to oxygen and the ethanol oxidises. Very often the last litre (2 pints) or so out of a cask that's been on sale too long will display this note, the next stage being vinegar! When a beer is young and just out of the fermenter there is still some final fermentation activity taking place, which is why it's always best to leave a beer to finish off or mature for another few days. During this time the acetaldehyde is converted to alcohol. A rush to chill and rack off the beer may mean that there's insufficient yeast around to finish the conversion process. Finally there are a couple of strains of bacteria that can also produce the compound so it's worth reviewing your hygiene regime if all else has been done properly.

TIP 385: *Butterscotch belongs in a sweet shop, not a brewery*

⚫ Butterscotch is another common taint and is sometimes described as buttery or even milky. It's diacetyl. In small quantities it can certainly enhance particular styles of ale but in excess, or in a lager, it is not desirable. The usual reason for excess diacetyl is lack of yeast contact during the final stages of fermentation/maturation. As with acetaldehyde there's still a degree of yeast metabolism needed to tidy up and finish the fermentation off. Don't rush to cool your beer ready for racking once primary fermentation appears to have finished. Instead, leave it for a further 24 hours. Indeed a low fermentation temperature can lead to yeast dropping out early so you might want to raise it to 18°C (64°F) for a day or so. This will bring the yeast back to life and clear up the diacetyl. Once again though, bacteria can also be the culprit.

TIP 386: *Sweetcorn goes with chicken, not with beer*

● This aroma has also been likened to that of tinned tomatoes, baked beans and even seaweed. It's caused by DMS – dimethyl sulphide. As with any sulphur compound it's not the nicest thing to have in most beer styles. Although it's an accepted characteristic of some styles of lager, it should never be overbearing. Root causes of DMS are usually using undermodified malts, particularly genuine lager malts, and a poor quality of boil. If necessary, extend your boil time to drive off excess DMS, making sure the boil is vigorous, and cool the wort quickly to stop further DMS being produced in the stand post-boil. Yeast can also produce DMS, as again can certain strains of bacteria.

TIP 387: *Avoid meaty notes in your beer*

● All the yeast will eventually die off, and when it does so a self-digestion process called autolysis kicks in. The cell contents are released through the cell walls out into the beer, which then picks up a meaty note. It's a characteristic of some well-aged bottled ales and certain Belgian styles where prolonged yeast contact is normal. As a rule of thumb, however, it's better to move the beer off the bulk of the yeast once all the main metabolic pathways are finished and into cool storage either in bottle, keg or cask. It's not such a problem when using dried yeast, but can be more of an issue in repitched but poor-quality wet yeast saved from an earlier fermentation.

TIP 388: *Learn to dodge stink bombs*

⚫ Remember stink bombs? Little glass capsules filled with sticky goo that stank of rotten eggs? Well, you can get stink bombs in your beer thanks to yet another sulphur compound, hydrogen sulphide. Not very pleasant at all, and again it comes down, in the main, to a couple of areas: yeast strain and bacteria. Almost all yeast strains will produce hydrogen sulphide as a by-product of amino acid metabolisation, but most of it is usually 'scrubbed' out by the CO_2 rising to the surface during fermentation. There are certain yeast strains, though, that produce it in abundance, so you might wish to switch strains. Highly sulphated water can also increase the production of hydrogen sulphide. It's also worth checking the fermentation temperature, pitching rate and wort aeration.

TIP 389: *Honey, sherry, cardboard, toffee and cat pee. Mmmmm!*

⚫ These are all generally derived from the effect of oxygen on beer, or more correctly from oxidation, and sometimes crop up if the beer has been over-aged. Unlike big commercial breweries, which can pretty much eliminate the exposure of finished beer to oxygen during packing, most home brewers can't use CO_2 or nitrogen blankets and purges when filling bottles, kegs or casks. And it only takes a thimbleful of air to ruin 500L (132 gallons) of beer! However, oxidation is not just caused by molecular oxygen alone. Oxidation is defined as a reaction process whereby a compound is given added oxygen or has hydrogen removed. Now, there are at least 1,000 identified compounds in the finished product, and probably loads more still waiting to be identified, that might be the cause of oxidation reactions. Don't let low ABV and light-coloured beers sit around: drink them fresh! However, some dark high-ABV beers will last for a couple of years, maybe longer, if looked after.

TIP 390: Blood in my beer?!

⚫ An unpleasant metallic taint in beer is often described as bloodlike. Others descriptors include "inky," "tinny," or like "sucking a penny" (not recommended!). The obvious place to look for the origins of this metallic note is the equipment itself. Some new vessels and pipework can often have a coating of dust from where it may have been worked or stored. Ensure that all new equipment is thoroughly washed with a light detergent to remove grease and dust and then rinsed thoroughly. Secondly, you may have a piece of worn or damaged kit with an exposed edge. Finally, it could be down to the water you use. Although unlikely, there may be a noticeable iron content or similar that could be the cause. Send off a sample for testing or speak to your supplier.

TIP 391: Herbal, spicy, clovelike and smoky: they can all be desirable aromas!

⚫ Some of these phenolic taints, like the cloves and spicy notes, are highly desirable in a wheat beer or smoked porter. Other times they're not so welcome. Most are produced by the yeast strain used in the fermentation, though common 'novice'-type errors, such as burning liquid sugar adjunct on the bottom of the kettle or the electric heating element, will most certainly give a smoked taint. One of the biggest culprits, and responsible in particular for the clovelike note, is wild yeast. This can come down to hygiene, but it also helps if you minimise the impact of the environment on your brewing. For example, don't leave or transfer uncovered beer near open windows.

TIP 392: *Beware boiled sweet, fruity and solvent aromas*

⚫ These are produced by ester compounds arising from a reaction between alcohol and acid. As with many things, esters can enhance a beer or be detrimental. So where do they come from? In general, it comes down to fermentation temperature: the warmer it is, the more likely the presence of esters. Another factor that can lead to increased esters is insufficient wort aeration.

TIP 393: *Watch out for vinegary aromas*

⚫ We've all had beer with a hint of vinegar to it, usually in an elderly cask ale, although kegs can pick it up from the dispense line. There are two causes: bacteria and oxidation. Bacteria can get into an open cask in a not-so-clean cellar or build up in gungy lines, so remember your hygiene. Make sure all vessels, taps, and lines are cleaned properly with the right solution before introducing them to your beer! Oxidation is the other source of vinegary notes; ethanol oxidises to acetaldehyde, which then oxidises to acetic acid. Don't leave you beer hanging around for too long once it's open.

TIP 394: *Defend your beer against bacteria*

⚫ Finally we come to bacteria and their possible effects on beer. From fermentation to the beer glass these little chaps can have a drastic effect on both beer quality and flavour. Fortunately for us, beer isn't actually the best environment for many of the nastier strains to inhabit. Beer is acidic, contains alcohol, and has no oxygen; these factors, along with the anti-bacterial nature of hop acids, make it unfavourable for the majority of bugs. However, there are three main strains that you should be aware of, whose overall effects are similar in that they all sour beer and cause haze. They are lactobacillus, pediococcus and acetobacter.

ESTIMATING ALCOHOL CONTENT

TIP 395: *Gravity is not the same as ABV*

⚫ At some point you're going to want to know how strong your beer actually is. This isn't too difficult and involves just a simple calculation involving the original gravity (OG), the final gravity (FG) and a conversion factor (0.13). For example, if we have a beer that started life with an OG of 1055 and finished with an FG of 1014 then the approximate percentage of alcohol by volume can be calculated as follows: (1055–1014) x 0.13 = 5.3%. There's a range of conversion factors used by commercial brewers and laid down by the government. These range from 0.128 upwards and depend on the OG of the beer involved but for our purposes 0.13 is fine.

TIP 396: *ABV is not the only measure of strength*

⚫ Degrees proof and proof are pretty much obsolete now, and although obscure calibrations such as Plato and Balling are sometimes used, percentage alcohol by volume is the most widely used measurement in the world. But not in the US beer market, which prefers percentage alcohol by weight. It's very similar, but the standard conversion factor is 1.2 rather than 0.13. Therefore the ABV of 5.3%, above, would equal 6.4% ABW.

THE TRANSITION BREWERY

Many microbrewers set up in business only after years as devoted home brewers. Often they graduated step by step from extract brewing in their kitchens to installing professional equipment in garages or outbuildings, and from then it was an easy transition into brewing full-time. In this chapter, we'll look at how you can set out on the same pathway without necessarily committing to going the whole hog.

ASSESSING AND PREPARING YOUR BUILDING

TIP 397: *Does your outbuilding measure up?*

⚫ It's time to move out of the kitchen and into a transition brewery located, for example, in the garage. You're going to be installing permanent vessels, and you'll need space. Not as much space as you might think – 3 x 3.5m (10 x 12ft) is perfectly adequate, and there are fully functioning commercial microbreweries that are even smaller than that (although, to be fair, they have to carry out quite a few procedures such as cask washing offsite). The important thing is that the space is entirely your own. You won't be competing with anyone else, and everything you need will be to hand, in its proper place, when you want to use it.

TIP 398: *If floor space is limited, go for height*

⚫ The best way to move liquids about is to let gravity do it for you, and the ideal layout for your equipment will be as much vertical as horizontal. A ceiling height of 3m (10ft) is probably too much to hope for, unless you have an outbuilding, such as a barn or a stable, that can be converted. Nevertheless, when designing your installation, position your racking and shelving to make the best possible use of the height you've got.

TIP 399: *Insulate it well*

As you already know, beer likes a steady temperature both during its secondary fermentation and in storage. The first thing you want to do to your brewhouse, then, is insulate it well. The ambient temperature should be around 12°C (54°F), during the night as well as during the day, to allow ales to condition comfortably. A shady spot away from extremes of sun and wind help, but you may not have the choice. In that case use plenty of insulation – not forgetting the ceiling! – and if necessary use fans during heatwaves and storage heaters in winter to maintain the temperature. Oh – and if you don't feel the need to wear a jumper while working in your brewery, it's probably too warm.

GUIDELINES IN BREWERY DESIGN

TIP 400: *Make a floor plan*

⚫ Cramming all the equipment into the space you're likely to have available – not to mention your storage and packaging areas – is probably not as easy as it might seem. Before parting with a single dollar, make an accurate floor plan, remembering to site your vessels so that you can clean all round them and with enough head clearance to allow room for inspection and, again, cleaning. And when shopping for new vessels, remember that tall, slender, cylindrical options take up least space.

TIP 401 *Pump it up!*

⚫ In a transition brewery you will be relying on pipes rather than buckets to transfer liquids between stages. And because you don't have the height to rely on gravity feed at all stages, you're going to need pumps. Pumps are also essential for drawing cleaning fluid through the pipework. Electric pumps are a bit fancy at this stage, but there are many brands of hand-operated siphoning diaphragm pump on the market.

TIP 402: *Make a diagram of pipes and pumps*

● Pipes and pumps all need to be unobtrusive yet easily accessible for repairing and cleaning. To this end, you'll need a practical blueprint of pipe routing and pump location. Pipework should be positioned out of your way while you're working, so clip all pipes securely to the wall or the rafters.

TIP 403: *Start with the floor*

● All floors in the brewery should be concrete, at least 15cm (6in) deep and either tiled (non-slip, of course!) or coated with a durable material that has a smooth flat surface that allows efficient cleaning and sanitation. Wall-to-floor joints should be skirted with the same material to a depth of at least 8cm (3in). The floor should have a 1–1.5% fall towards the drains to prevent pooling of water after hosing down/cleaning, and all drains should have the appropriate airlocks and be covered with baskets to retain any broken glass. The floors of the storage and packaging areas must be made from materials that resist acidic and caustic substances at the concentration levels used during the brewing process. In the areas earmarked for storage of chemical concentrates (acids, detergents, etc) the floors and walls should be resistant to damage resulting from exposure to them.

TIP 404: *Aim to have washable walls and ceilings*

⊛ The walls of the brewery itself should either be tiled to the ceiling or sealed with a durable and washable coating. Even the ceilings need a washable coating, and any exposed (ie, untiled) areas in the building – including the storage and packaging areas – should be painted with kitchen/bathroom mould-resistant paint. Steam abounds in a brewery, which causes condensation and therefore encourages mould!

TIP 405: *Make sure the brewery is well ventilated*

⊛ It's not just steam that needs to be vented; any buildup of CO_2 is dangerous and must be dispersed. An air conditioning system may be a little excessive, but an ordinary kitchen/bathroom extractor fan fitted to the window will be invaluable, even if the building has a good air flow (unlikely in a garage!). Alternatively – and assuming you're handy in such matters – an ordinary cooker hood with extractor can be fitted over the FV.

TIP 406: *Watch out for dust traps and insects*

⊛ No protrusions should be allowed on the walls of the brewhouse, and the windowsills should be outside not in! If that's impossible, any internal protrusions or beams or sills should have a 30° fall to prevent dust from accumulating. Any holes through to the exterior should be covered by plastic mosquito netting to keep insects, vermin, dirt and dust outside where they belong.

TIP 407: *Lay on hot running water as well as cold*

⚫ You don't need to be told that your brewery needs running water; it will use about five times as much cooling and cleaning water as brewing liquor. In truth, hot running water isn't absolutely essential because the first piece of equipment you install will be the hot liquor tank, which should supply enough hot water for all aspects of the brewing process. But the brewery will need a kitchen sink, and it's just so much more convenient to have a hot tap for washing your hands and soaking utensils. So go for it, if you can.

TIP 408: *Plan now for your effluent treatment*

⚫ What flows in must flow out, and although the effluent from home brewing isn't regulated, in most jurisdictions the effluent from commercial breweries most certainly is. So if this really is your transition brewery – your stepping stone to a very different life – have an eye to the future and plan now for the effluent treatment measures you're going to need one day. If you have a garden pond, or space for one, you might consider turning it into a reedbed. The theory is that *Phragmites australis*, the common reed, oxygenates the water sufficiently to host a population of bacteria that will digest the proteins and pathogens (if any) in your waste water. There are, however, drawbacks, not least the cost of installing them, the space they take up, the maintenance they require and the risk of pollution associated with them. For these reasons, they are falling out of favour with brewers.

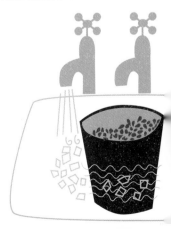

TIP 409: *Do it the French way*

⚫ An alternative is the sand trap, which is the standard method of effluent treatment in rural France, where most houses have septic tanks. This is a 1m- (3ft-) deep sandpit on a base of fine gravel. In the sand is buried a very long coil of durable perforated hose connected to a holding tank in the brewery in which the solids in your effluent – mainly hop sediment – are allowed to settle out pre-discharge. The sandpit soon builds up a population of bacteria that feed on the proteins and other solids in your effluent, and the water emerges clean enough to go into the common drain or a handy watercourse. Don't use bleach in this sort of system, though: it kills the very bacteria you want to encourage.

TIP 410: *Three-phase electricity will save you money*

⚫ Even if you opt for a gas-fired copper (boiler; see Tip 417, page 215), you're going to use a lot of electricity. You'll have your hot liquor tank, your copper, your temperature-controlled lagering tanks and storage, your ordinary heating and lighting, any pumps you might install – the list goes on, and the arrival of the monthly utilities bill could easily become problematic. So switch to three-phase electricity. A single-phase supply uses 120–130 amps to generate 36kW of heat, whereas three-phase supply draws only half that. It also means you can happily turn on every machine you own without blowing the fuses – always a comfort!

TIP 411: *You'll probably need professional help*

● You are required by law to use a licenced electrician to wire your brewery and to install and maintain any fixed electrical equipment – just as you might when fitting out a kitchen. And pretty much wherever you are, if you're connecting to the gas supply you will need a professional to do the initial job and then to check it annually. You should always check that your tradesperson holds a valid licence for the job at hand before you hire.

TIP 412: *Use gravity where you can*

● In an ideal world you'd make use of gravity for every transfer of liquids, especially hot ones, but the building you're adapting is very unlikely to have the height to allow you to fit a true tower brewery. If you can use gravity, though, plan your racking and shelving to have as many steps as the ceiling height permits bearing in mind two things: you need sufficient headroom to be able to inspect and clean them thoroughly; and if possible your mash tun and copper should be on upper stages so that you can discharge them by gravity. Having to pump out your mash tun will complicate the sparging process. Also, you want to run off your hopped wort as splashily as you can to help re-aerate it after the boil.

EQUIPPING THE TRANSITION BREWERY

TIP 413: *You really need a hot liquor tank*

⊛ Up to now you may well have been making your brewpot or boiler double up as a hot liquor tank. However, once you're brewing greater quantities, and probably more frequently too, the convenience of a separate hot liquor tank makes it pretty much indispensable. It needs a thermostat so that you can either boil water when you're treating it or get it up to just the right temperature for mashing and sparging and hold it there for as long as you need. For American home brewers in particular, a three-phase or industrial electricity supply (see Tip 410, page 212) is now crucial; you can't run an electric hot liquor tank on 110 volts!

TIP 414: *Switch to a cylindrical mash tun*

⊛ Until now you've probably been using an adapted coolbox as a mash tun, and there's nothing wrong with that. But now you're equipping your temporary brewery, which could – if you ever decided to make that leap – take you over the threshold into the very much more intense world of commercial brewing. You may therefore want something a little more sophisticated, which is easy to operate but efficient. A cylindrical or drum-shaped vessel will hold more than twice the volume of a box of the same surface area, so a cylindrical mash tun will lose heat much more slowly than a box of the same volume, making your extraction more efficient.

TIP 415: *Fit a rotating sparge arm*

⬤ Sparging is an operation that, at this stage in your development as a brewer, you will want to take for granted. So fit a rotating sparge arm to your shiny new mash tun. It almost goes without saying that the rotating arm you fit will work far more effectively in a drum than in a box – no corners to miss! – increasing the efficiency of the process.

TIP 416: *Your new copper: time to choose!*

⬤ Most British home brewers, thanks to the 230V domestic electricity supply, will likely have opted initially for electric boilers heated by kettle or immersion heater elements. Now that you're moving into your transition brewery, you should look again at the options available. All have advantages and disadvantages and, given how much you might be about to spend, now is the time to make that once-and-for-all decision.

TIP 417: *Weigh up the pros and cons of gas*

⬤ Gas-fired coppers are available in all sizes and prices, and can be run off bottles or the mains. One advantage over electric coppers is that they can be turned on to warm up in advance of the run-off from the mash tun; another is that (as every cook will tell you!) gas is more responsive than electricity, since there are no elements that have to warm up or cool down. A feature of direct-fired coppers – and it's either an advantage or a disadvantage, depending on who you talk to – is the formation of caramel on the localised hotspots created by the burners. These patches need special attention when cleaning!

TIP 418: *Electricity is cleaner*

⚫ The great advantage of the electric copper is that there are no naked flames involved, so it's both cleaner and safer than gas. It's cost-efficient too, except that you have to run 7–10cm (3–4in) of wort over the elements before you can even turn them on, so it's slower to bring the wort to the boil. Maintenance might be more of an issue, especially as you have to be a qualified electrician before you can do so much as unsheathe a screwdriver. But if you do opt for electric, remember to keep plenty of spare heating elements handy.

TIP 419: *Steam is clean and controllable*

⚫ Many large commercial breweries heat their boilers by using steam that circulates through jackets built into the walls of their coppers. It's a great system in many ways: it distributes the heat evenly; it doesn't cause scorching or caramelisation; and it can be turned on and off instantly. You can do this too, by fitting a steam-release valve and pipe connector to the lid of your hot liquor tank, although it is a complicated business. You will need to calculate the length of piping you'll need to bring your wort to the boil and how great a volume of steam you'll need for a 90-minute boil. You don't want your boiler to run dry, but then you don't want to have to top it up halfway through the boil either.

TIP 420: *Bear steam in mind for the future*

⬤ Switching to steam might be a step too far at this stage but, if you're planning an expandable brewery for the future, it's worth designing the pipework and layout with steam in mind, because a ready supply of steam has two other valuable functions. Steam under pressure is ideal for cleaning the insides of kegs and barrels, especially wooden ones, and a bubble pipe in your mash tun will enable you to do all sorts of fancy things with your mash temperature without excessive dilution of the mash.

TIP 421: *Steam and safety*

⬤ One warning, though: steam – the steam that will scald you – is invisible but will give you a much nastier burn than boiling water. What you can actually see is only water vapour recondensing on contact with the cooler air. But if you have a pinhole leak in a hose or a pipe you might very well not see any vapour, and the first you'll know of the leak is when you reach across the pipework for a spanner or a cup of tea and the underside of your forearm is suddenly – and possibly badly – scalded. Avoid this through thorough maintenance, and reduce the risk further by using the steam only under low pressure.

TIP 422: *Switch to external cooling rings*

⬤ For reasons of hygiene, it's best to keep the attemperator (the immersion coil) out of the wort and, wherever possible, have it fitted externally. By this stage in your development, two rings (top and bottom) are better than one. Always start cooling with the top ring, then bring the lower one into play at 10°C (50°F) to achieve the lowest temperature possible for your system. This promotes convection currents, and therefore a more even cooling.

TIP 423: *Get a remote*

⚫ Remote chillers are used in pub and bar cellars to supply cooling to both the beer and the beer lines on the way to the point of dispense via what is commonly called a 'python'. This is a thick bundle of beer lines in a single outer sheath inside which a cold water line and return are fed. The remote chiller consists of a cooling/refrigeration unit and pump. Reconditioned models can be picked up for a reasonable price and are nowadays programmable, so it's possible to set it at whatever temperatures you want. Simply connect the outlet and return inlet to the cooling rings on the FV, set the temperature and switch it all on. A single cellar-size remote chiller should be able to handle 400–1,000L (100–265 gallons) of wort comfortably from 25°C (77°F) down to 10°C (50°F) in a matter of hours. Smaller under-the-counter flash coolers do the same job and would be great for smaller lots of up to 200L (50 gallons) but these, in general, aren't programmable so a timer might be advisable.

TIP 424: *Upgrade to a paraflow*

⚫ Depending on the size of your new brewery, though, you're likely to find that a coil-based system of any description is no longer up to the job of cooling your hopped wort. Remember, it really needs to get down to pitching temperature within half an hour of flame out if you're to get that vital cold break; and if you're brewing in any quantity only a counterflow or paraflow can be guaranteed to do the trick. Because the hot wort and cold water run against each other, the wort spends more time in contact with the water than would otherwise be the case and therefore cools more rapidly.

TIP 425: *Make it a big paraflow*

⚫ Some metal-bashing fanatics build their own, but you needn't; even a small shop-bought paraflow – one that claims to cool 500L (132 gallons) an hour – isn't terribly expensive and should be pretty reliable in action. Don't, however, automatically buy the smallest: the bigger the paraflow, the quicker it will work. So if you can afford it, buy a bigger one than you need at present; it'll give you peace of mind, and it's one more item to tick off your list if you decide to make the transition to commercial brewing.

TIP 426: *Don't throw away your immersion coil*

⚫ In some places and at some times of year, the supposedly cold tap water is actually tepid – 25°C (77°F) or possibly even more. Brackish water running through your paraflow simply won't cool your wort to pitching temperature, so rescue the immersion coil you so cruelly discarded, sit it in one of your many brewing buckets, fill the bucket with as much ice as you can come by, and hook it up to your water supply at one end and the paraflow at the other. Abracadabra – you've got a pre-chiller!

TIP 427: *Save energy – recycle your cooling fluid*

⚫ The water coming out of the paraflow will be surprisingly warm, having absorbed most of the heat from the hopped wort. That's heat you've paid for via your utility bills – don't waste it! Instead of pouring it down the drain, run it off into your hot liquor tank and boil it to be your next batch of treated brewing liquor.

TIP 428: *Now's the time for all those checks and tests*

⚫ Remember Chapter 8 on troubleshooting? In your old kitchen-based brewery, your hopped wort was either in the boiler/brewpot or in an intermediate vessel, a wort cooler, getting chilled with your immersion coil. And it was at this point that you tested the pH, gravity and clarity and made all the necessary adjustments. Now that you're the proud owner of a paraflow, you'll have run your hopped wort directly into the fermenter and you'll want to pitch it and get the lid on safely as quickly as possible. Don't worry, though; there's still time for the necessary tests, provided you have everything you might need to hand – litmus papers, hydrometer/refractometer, acidity adjusters and sugar or DME syrup.

TIP 429: *Strapped for space? Try the Russian Doll*

⚫ It's all very well investing in increasingly large pieces of kit, but none of it is much use if you don't have the room for it. There is an alternative. The Russian Doll system consists of a single electric boiler with a hoist mounted above it. First it's your hot liquor/water treatment tank; next it's your mash tun. When you have treated the water and got it to strike temperature, attach to the hoist either a grain bag or, better, a close-mesh metal basket containing the grist. When the liquor's cool enough, lower the bag or basket into it, seal it all up and let it mash. When it's mashed, lift the bag/basket out and sparge it, if necessary, while it's still suspended over the boiler. Then it's your copper – simply bring it to the boil and go through your hopping routine, using bags for the hops. Finally, the same vessel is your wort cooler – get the immersion coil into it again, with additional ice bottles if necessary, and get the wort down to pitching temperature before running it off into your FV.

TIP 430: *Build your own Russian Doll...*

🌑 A Russian Doll is simplicity itself to build. The only item that would need to be improvised or fabricated is the hoist, which can either be freestanding, and preferably on casters, or built into the ceiling. At this stage of your brewing career it won't be required to bear much weight, so a perfectly ordinary laundry rack, suitably adapted, will almost certainly be robust enough for the job. After all, a week's wash still wet from the machine is bound to weigh more than the spent grains of a single mash.

TIP 431: *... Or buy a posh one*

🌑 There are a number of commercial systems of varying degrees of sophistication on the market, such as the Speidel Braumeister from Germany. These were designed with the small bar owner in mind, and are planned to give the greatest yield for the lowest input of time and effort. This particular brand is almost fully automated, allowing you to preset times and temperatures for your mash and boil; all you have to do is make up the grist, dunk it into the liquor, lift it out again and be on hand for your hop additions. It comes in 20L (5-gallon), 50L (13-gallon) and 200L (53-gallon) capacities.

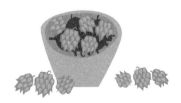

TIP 432: *Get a bigger FV than you need*

No matter how much you plan to brew in the short term, it's always a good idea to get a fermenting vessel that's bigger than you need. Of course, this will allow plenty of headspace, but it will also allow you to expand the brewing operation in the future. The classic way to expand a brewery is to add more and bigger conditioning tanks as and when you need them; if you've already got a big enough fermenter to start with, you won't have to replace it later on. It doesn't have to take up that much space, either: a 400L (106-gallon) tank that's 1.5m (5ft) tall has a diameter of only 74cm (2ft 5in).

TIP 433: *Build temperature control into your lagering tanks*

It's not so difficult to maintain the correct temperature for fermenting your ales – it's pretty much the same as room temperature. Lager is different, though. Its primary fermentation, which can last from 3–5 weeks, requires a temperature of 7°C (45°F), although anything up to 12°C (54°F) is permissible. It then needs to condition for 4–5 weeks at 7°C or, better still, 60–90 days at 2°C (36°F). Those temperatures really ought to be pretty constant, and holding them down at that level can be a challenge. A popular option with the more practical-minded home brewers is to build a plywood cabinet, line it with builder's insulating sheets and install an electric heat exchanger such as a Peltier unit controlled by a temperature probe. The disadvantage of this method for the transition brewery – apart from the fact that you need quite a high level of skill to construct it – is that it's inflexible. Every time you want to expand production, you have to build another cabinet. It's better, therefore, to cool each tank individually.

TIP 434: *Dig out the immersion coil(s) again*

⬤ Holding your lager at 2°C (36°F) for so long is probably too much of a challenge for most home brewers, and the quicker option of 7°C (45°F) for 4–5 weeks, although perhaps less authentic, is more easily achievable. For tanks of up to 100L (26½ gallons), first use your immersion coil and an ice bucket to get your coolant down to near zero. Next, either immerse a second coil in the tank or wrap a second and very much longer coil of hose closely around your lagering tank and feed the very cold water from the first coil into it. A thermal probe built into the lid of the tank will tell you when the beer has hit the required temperature. If your tank is well enough insulated and stored in a cool place, it should stay cold for a good long time. Check the temperature regularly and repeat the chilling process as necessary. You can also add more insulation if the temperature doesn't seem to be holding. Bigger tanks would need much more elaborate cooling systems, but if you're planning on making more than 100L of lager at a time, you're probably better off at this stage adding more 100L tanks to your array rather than buying a single giant tank.

TIP 435: *Equip yourself for large-scale bottling*

⬤ Bottling batches of 100L (26½ gallons) at a time is a task of an entirely different order from what you're used to. Yes, you can be patient and fill 200 bottles one at a time – in a meditative, 'zen' kind of way it might even be a pleasure – but soaking and washing 200 bottles in anything less than the biggest batches you can manage is unconscionable.

TIP 436: Soak and rinse in a cheap plastic FV

⬤ The cheapest 120L (32-gallon) plastic FV is ideal for soaking and rinsing for two reasons. (1) It has a flush lid, which – if you fill it right to the brim – will hold the bottles completely underwater and thus ensure that all of them come into full contact with the cleaning agent. (2) It has an outflow tap, meaning that, to rinse your bottles after their soak, you need only stand the bucket in the sink, open the tap, take the lid off and give the contents a good long shower under sufficient pressure to force the detergent and solid residue out and clean water in. The bottles should be layered upright in the FV, not on their sides or with their mouths facing downward, or you'll get airlocks in them and the detergent won't come into contact with all the interior surfaces. Annoyingly, the 120L plastic FV in the cheapest range available won't quite hold 200 500ml (1 pint) bottles. Luckily, the next size up (210L; 55 gallons) has a diameter of less than 60cm (2ft) so won't take up too much space and, of course, has a multiplicity of uses – not least as an FV!

TIP 437: Take the smart option – sanitise in the same FV!

⬤ You don't even need to remove the bottles from the FV before stage two in your bottle-washing procedure – simply fill the FV with your sodium metabisulphite solution and leave it for half an hour – as you know, sodium metabisulphite doesn't need rinsing as it dissipates naturally. After this, you'll need one additional piece of equipment – a bottle tree – to drain all the clean bottles on. There should be no need to dry them.

TIP 438: *Use a simple bottle filler*

● There are several inexpensive models of bottle filler on the market
that consist of little more than a bottling bucket, three or four spouts,
and a fill-level valve that you can preset. They operate by siphon action,
automatically stopping at the correct level, and it's claimed they are able
to fill 200 500ml (1 pint) bottles in an hour. There are very much more
elaborate bottle fillers available, which are fitted with electric pumps
and electronic fill level control, but they are much more expensive and
not actually that much faster.

TIP 439: *Bottle and cap a few at a time*

● Although there are plenty of fancy bottle fillers on the market that
are suitable for home brewers, there is no suitable alternative to closing
the bottles, whether by cap or by cork, one at a time. If you're anxious
about leaving open bottles of beer standing around for any length of
time – and you should be! – then pause every time you've filled a dozen
or so and close them. But to speed the job up and make it more bearable,
you're still better off following Marvin and Kim's advice: it takes two!

BEER STYLES
AND RECIPES

This chapter provides a fairly representative selection of recipes drawn from a wide range of sources. For the novice, sticking as closely as possible to the recipes will usually produce a pretty decent beer and will also provide a foundation of knowledge of most beer styles on which to build. For the old hand, a recipe is no more than an adventure playground for the brewing imagination!

BRITISH ALES

It's important to note that all the recipes in the following three sections require an ale yeast strain.

TIP 440: *Make a checklist*

 No matter how many times you brew and how experienced you feel you are there's always the risk of distraction, which increases the probability that you'll overlook a mundane but essential part of the process. Having a simple checklist to hand, with items for you to tick off as you progress, is a great way of ensuring you don't forget to do anything important. From treating the water through to pitching the yeast, the list acts as a failsafe to make sure that everything you need is ready and waiting, exactly when you need it, and that no step in the procedure has been missed out.

All the recipes that follow are formulated for full-grain mashes. Extracts are more concentrated and indeed might even be called 'concentrate' – substitute 750g (26½oz) of liquid extract or 625g (22oz) of dried extract for every 1kg (2⅕lb) of malt.

TIP 441: *Bitter*

⬤ Until it was overtaken by lager in the 1980s, bitter had been the British drinker's go-to beer for nearly half a century. Bitter evolved from pale ale after World War I as a classier alternative to mild, which was the working man's staple, and by the 1950s there was usually a choice of three strengths: 'session', or 'ordinary', at (very roughly) 3.6–4% ABV; 'best', from 4–4.5%, and 'strong', or 'special', from 4.5–5%. The stronger bitters were sometimes called 'Burton' in order to associate themselves with England's brewing capital, and some breweries only produced them in winter. Young's Winter Warmer at 5%, for instance, was originally marketed as Young's Burton Ale.

TOTAL LIQUOR: 35L (9¼ gallons)

Ingredients: 3.7kg (8⅛lb) pale malt • 200g (7oz) crystal malt

MASH LIQUOR: 10L (2½ gallons)

MASH TIME: 90 minutes

MASH TEMP: 66°C (151°F)

BOIL: 90 minutes

HOPS: 21g (¾oz) Progress, 21g Whitbread Goldings at start of boil; 14g (½oz) Whitbread Goldings at 80 minutes

EST. OG: 1036 EST. ABV: 3.6%

TIP 442: *Best bitter*

 Nowadays, it's less common to hear someone ordering a pint of 'best' in a British pub – that belongs to the days when pubs only sold the brewery's own range of beers. There are still many fine best bitters brewed in Britain, but they now have brand names: Fuller's London Pride, Charles Wells Bombardier and Marston's Pedigree are among the best-known British ales.

TOTAL LIQUOR: 35L (9¼ gallons)

Ingredients: 4.5kg (10lb) pale malt • 240g (8½oz) crystal malt

MASH LIQUOR: 12L (3⅕ gallons)

MASH TIME: 90 minutes

MASH TEMP: 66°C (151°F)

BOIL: 90 minutes

HOPS: 35g (1¼oz) Challenger at start of boil

EST. OG: 1043 EST. ABV: 4.4%

TIP 443: *Special bitter*

⬤ Special or strong bitters, such as the renowned British ale Greene King Abbot Ale, date back to the late 1950s and early 1960s, when Britain's economy started to recover in earnest after the war. Better-off customers could now afford a stronger, more characterful tipple from time to time, and with wartime restrictions on supplies of barley for malting being lifted in 1953, the brewers were able to provide it.

TOTAL LIQUOR: 36L (9½ gallons)

Ingredients: 4.5kg (10lb) pale malt • 540g (19oz) torrefied wheat • 400g (14oz) white sugar • 400g crystal malt • 110g (3⅘oz) chocolate malt (optional)

MASH LIQUOR: 14L (3⅔ gallons)

MASH TIME: 90 minutes

MASH TEMP: 66°C (151°F)

BOIL TIME: 90 minutes

HOPS: 28g (approx. 1oz) Challenger, 28g Progress, 14g (½oz) Fuggle at start of boil; 20g (¾oz) Goldings at 80 minutes

EST. OG 1056 EST ABV: 6%

TIP 444: *Golden ale*

⊛ Many British breweries, especially in the northwest of England, traditionally produced very light-bodied and very pale bitters for industrial workers. The best known was Boddington's, a session bitter at 3.8% ABV, but others, such as Wem Pale, were closer to light milds. However, in the 1990s a new style of golden ale was identified (see *Journal of the Institute of Brewing 1995*). These new golden ales were generally stronger at 4–5% ABV and were typified by greater use of aromatic hop varieties than had been usual in British brewing. Originated and produced by microbreweries such as Hop Back and Oakham, they were aimed squarely at lager drinkers and sometimes contained a proportion of wheat malt to lighten the body. The style became popular very rapidly not only in Britain but in America too, where light grists and very aromatic hop strains were already common.

TOTAL LIQUOR: 36L (9½ gallons)

Ingredients: 5.5kg (12lb) pale malt

MASH LIQUOR: 13.5L (3½ gallons)

MASH TIME: 90 minutes

MASH TEMP: 66°C (151°F)

BOIL TIME: 90 minutes

HOPS: 50g (1¾oz) Challenger at start of boil; 18g (⅔oz) Goldings at 80 minutes; 10g (⅓oz) Goldings post-boil.

EST. OG: 1049 EST. ABV: 5%

TIP 445: American golden ale

🌐 A very light-bodied, refreshing ale with a terrific sting of aromatic hops. Citra or Chinook may be substituted for Galaxy and Cascade for Wai-iti, depending on availability.

TOTAL LIQUOR: 32L (8½ gallons)

Ingredients: 4kg (8⅘lb) pale malt • 500g (17⅔oz) Pilsner malt

MASH LIQUOR: 12L (3⅕ gallons)

MASH TIME: 60 minutes

MASH TEMP: 65°C (149°F)

BOIL TIME: 70 minutes

HOPS: 28g (approx. 1oz) Galaxy at start of boil; 28g Galaxy and 28g Wai-iti at flame out

YEAST: American ale

EST. OG: 1046 EST. ABV: 4.5%

TIP 446: *India pale ale*

● India pale ales (IPAs), like Porter (see Tip 456, page 244), were principally intended as export beers. In order to withstand the long voyage around the Cape of Good Hope they were very heavily hopped and were commonly put to sea as soon as their primary fermentation had ceased. The long secondary fermentation in cask in the holds of the clippers that carried them generated enough CO_2 to protect them in transit; but there is no evidence to suggest that they were unusually strong, as was once thought. New evidence also shows that while 'company men' (East India Company managers and officials), officers in the East India Company's army and 'box wallahs' (civilian tradespeople) enjoyed their IPA, the lower ranks stuck firmly to their porter!

TOTAL LIQUOR: 33L (8½ gallons)

Ingredients: 6kg (13⅕lb) pale malt • 140g (5oz) crystal malt

MASH LIQUOR: 14L (3⅔ gallons)

MASH TIME: 60 minutes

MASH TEMP: 65°C (149°F)

BOIL TIME: 70 minutes

HOPS: 70g (2½oz) Challenger at start of boil; 35g (1¼oz) Goldings at 55 minutes; 35g Goldings at flame out

EST. OG: 1060 EST. ABV: 5.7%

TIP 447: Dark mild

'Mild' is one of the oldest designators in British brewing history, going back to Saxon times. But mild as we know it was a beer for industrial workers: dark (usually), sweet (by comparison) and highly calorific, it was just what you needed after a 10-hour shift. At first it wasn't necessarily weaker than pale ale or bitter, but it was less assertively hopped. The usual alcohol content only dropped to its present 3–3.5% ABV in the first 30 years of the 20th century when a combination of wartime malting restrictions, high unemployment and aggressive temperance campaigning led to a general reduction in the alcoholic strength of British beers. It lost its dominance in the 1950s when better pay allowed drinkers to 'upgrade' to bitter. By the 1990s it had almost disappeared and awaits a revival.

TOTAL LIQUOR: 34L (9 gallons)

Ingredients: 3kg (6²⁄₃lb) pale malt • 450g (15⁴⁄₅oz) crystal malt • 250g (8⁴⁄₅oz) black malt • 140g (5oz) flaked wheat

MASH LIQUOR: 9.5L (2½ gallons)

MASH TIME: 90 minutes

MASH TEMP: 67°C (153°F)

BOIL TIME: 90 minutes

HOPS: 28g (approx. 1oz) Challenger at start of boil; 10g (⅓oz) Goldings at 80 minutes

EST. OG: 1033 EST. ABV: 3.1%

TIP 448: *Light mild*

● British mild ales were generally dosed with flavourful coloured malts to compensate for their low alcohol content. But in many rural areas light milds or 'boy's bitters' were once just as popular among farm workers who, especially at haymaking and harvest time, spent the whole day toiling in the sunshine and needed rehydration – and fast!

TOTAL LIQUOR: 35L (9¼ gallons)

Ingredients: 4kg (8⁴⁄₅lb) pale malt • 28g (approx. 1oz) crystal malt

MASH LIQUOR: 10L (2⅔ gallons)

MASH TIME: 90 minutes

MASH TEMP: 67°C (153°F)

BOIL TIME: 90 minutes

HOPS: 30g (approx. 1oz) Goldings at start of boil; 10g (⅓oz) Goldings at 80 minutes

EST. OG: 1036 EST. ABV: 3.6%

TIP 449: *Strong mild*

Before World War I strong milds were common in many industrial areas. The style died out due to wartime malt restrictions and high duty. The economic problems of the 1920s and '30s prevented them from making a comeback until microbrewers rediscovered them in the 1990s. There are now many fine examples of these rich, smooth and luscious beers being brewed and enjoyed.

TOTAL LIQUOR: 36L (9$\frac{1}{2}$ gallons)

Ingredients: 5.5kg (12lb) pale malt • 1kg (2$\frac{1}{5}$lb) crystal malt

MASH LIQUOR: 16L (4$\frac{1}{4}$ gallons)

MASH TIME: 90 minutes

MASH TEMP: 67°C (153°F)

BOIL TIME: 90 minutes

HOPS: 30g (approx. 1oz) Fuggle, 30g Goldings at start of boil; 20g (⅔oz) Fuggle at 80 minutes

EST. OG: 1058 EST. ABV: 5.7%

TIP 450: *Strong brown ale*

🍺 Brown ale was originally no more than bottled mild or porter. But after World War I, when mild ale became weaker and weaker and porter died out completely, strong brown ale survived and thrived in the north of England. This was because bottled beers were more expensive than draught and therefore had some social cachet: a bottle of brown was therefore, unlike a pint of mild, a treat. This recipe, incidentally, makes an excellent base for chestnut beer (see Tips 163 & 164, pages 90 & 91).

TOTAL LIQUOR: 32L (8½ gallons)

Ingredients: 4.8kg (10⅜lb) pale malt • 250g (8⅘oz) crystal malt • 100g (3½oz) chocolate malt

MASH LIQUOR: 27L (7 gallons)

MASH TIME: 60 minutes

MASH TEMP: 65°C (149°F)

BOIL TIME: 70 minutes

HOPS: 16g (⅗oz) Admiral at start of boil; 16g Challenger at flame out

YEAST: English ale strain

EST. OG: 1052 EST. ABV: 5%

STOUT AND PORTER

TIP 451: Dry stout

⚫ The term 'stout' originally designated a strong porter and, from the 19th century, stouts were regarded as luxury beers. Two styles evolved, dry and sweet. The sweet stouts were generally of low gravity, and as they were mostly sold as bottled beers (which were more expensive), they were widely regarded as drinks for working-class women being treated to a rare night out. They have now virtually died out, with Mackeson's (a 'milk' stout dosed with lactose) almost the last of the breed. Dry stouts, being much more bitter thanks to the use of roasted barley, were seen as more masculine. Most breweries produced a version, but because only Irish stout brewers were exempted from malting restrictions in World War I, they managed to monopolise the postwar market. Guinness in particular targeted the UK market and even built a brewery in London (now closed), and most UK breweries bottled it for sale in their pubs. Dry stouts are therefore now commonly called 'Irish' stout.

TOTAL LIQUOR: 32L (8½ gallons)

Ingredients: 3.4kg (7½lb) pale malt • 1kg (2⅕lb) flaked barley • 480g (17oz) roasted barley

MASH LIQUOR: 12L (3⅕ gallons)

MASH TIME: 90 minutes

MASH TEMP: 66°C (151°F)

BOIL TIME: 90 minutes

HOPS: 40g (1⅖oz) Target at start of boil

EST. OG: 1042 EST. ABV: 3.8%

TIP 452: *Milk stout*

Milk stout never, of course, contained milk; but it did contain the non-fermentable milk sugar lactose to create a sweet, soft-flavoured beer that was particularly favoured by women. Eventually the designation was banned as misleading, but lactose is still a valuable addition to any brewer's storecupboard.

TOTAL LIQUOR: 32L (8½ gallons)

Ingredients: 4.2kg (9¼lb) pale malt • 400g (14oz) chocolate malt • 400g crystal malt • 200g (7oz) roasted barley • 200g flaked barley

MASH LIQUOR: 13.5L (3½ gallons)

MASH TIME: 60 minutes

MASH TEMP: 67°C (153°F)

BOIL TIME: 75 minutes

HOPS: Challenger 28g (approx. 1oz) at start of boil; Goldings 11g (²⁄₅oz) at 60 minutes; lactose 850g (30oz) at 65 minutes

EST. OG: 1059 EST. ABV: 5.2%

TIP 453: *Oatmeal stout*

⬤ Cooked rolled oats are gelatinous and full of lipids, which is why porridge is so deliciously glutinous. Added to beer, especially stout, they affect the mouthfeel rather than the flavour and create a velvety smoothness.

TOTAL LIQUOR: 32L (8½ gallons)

Ingredients: 4.2kg (9¼lb) pale malt • 250g (8⅘lb) rolled oats
• 200g (7oz) crystal malt • 160g (5⅔oz) chocolate malt
• 70g (2½oz) roasted barley

MASH LIQUOR: 12L (3⅕ gallons)

MASH TIME: 60 minutes

MASH TEMP: 67°C (153°F)

BOIL TIME 70 minutes

HOPS: Challenger 40g (1⅖oz) at start of boil; Challenger 16g (½oz), Golding 16g at flame out

EST. OG: 1049 EST. ABV: 4.6%

241

TIP 454: *Extra stout*

🌑 Stout, when first used to designate a beer style, meant strong rather than fat, and the first stouts were actually called stout porter. An extra stout is stronger still, but should not be as vinous as an old ale of the same strength. Guinness still brews its Extra (or Foreign Extra) Stout, which despite its alcoholic content has a certain quenching astringency.

TOTAL LIQUOR: 33L (8¾ gallons)

Ingredients: 4.5kg (10lb) pale malt • 1kg (2⅕lb) brown malt
• 450g (1lb) wheat malt • 450g flaked barley
• 250g (8⅘oz) crystal malt • 250g roasted barley
• 170g (6oz) chocolate malt • 170g black malt

MASH LIQUOR: 19L (5 gallons)

MASH TIME: 60 minutes

MASH TEMP: 68°C (154°F)

BOIL TIME: 90 minutes

HOPS: 100% Fuggle: 28g (approx. 1oz) at start of boil; 14g (½oz) at 30 minutes; 14g at 75 minutes

EST. OG: 1074 EST. ABV: 7.1%

TIP 455: Imperial stout

⬤ Strong, well-hopped porters and stouts were the first beers brewed with long-distance transport and, especially, export markets in mind (hence the name porter). In the early 18th century the Baltic ports were among Britain's busiest trading hubs, and porters and stouts quickly found favour there. Very strong stouts of 10% ABV and more were ordered by the Russian court in St Petersburg, and were therefore crowned with the title 'Imperial'.

TOTAL LIQUOR: 35L (9¼ gallons)

Ingredients: 7kg (1²/₅lb) pale malt • 700g (24²/₃oz) crystal malt • 200g (7oz) roasted barley • 150g (5¼oz) chocolate malt

MASH LIQUOR: 20L (5¼ gallons)

MASH TIME: 60 minutes

MASH TEMP: 65°C (149°F)

BOIL TIME: 75 minutes

HOPS: 56g (2oz) Challenger at start of boil; 56g Golding at 45 minutes

EST. OG: 1080 EST. ABV: 8.2%

TIP 456: *Porter*

● The first mass producers of beer in the world were not brewers *per se*; they were the malt distillers of early 18th-century London who, in 1700, brewed more than 8,000,000 gallons of malt liquor (wash) to make gin with, easily outproducing the city's beer brewers. Forty years later the malt distillers were brewing more than 60 million gallons of wash, and the engineering skills they had developed to build the vast FVs and conditioning tanks they needed – all coopered – had filtered through to the brewing industry. These developments in engineering enabled the brewers to produce their mid-strength brown beers in bulk, and casking them with plenty of condition and a heavy dose of hops meant they could export them by sea.

TOTAL LIQUOR: 33L (8¾ gallons)

Ingredients: 4.5kg (10lb) pale malt • 750g (26½oz) brown malt • 600g (21⅕oz) crystal malt • 120g (4¼oz) chocolate malt

MASH LIQUOR: 15L (4 gallons)

MASH TIME: 90 minutes

MASH TEMP: 66°C (151°F)

BOIL TIME: 90 minutes

HOPS: 100% Fuggle: 70g (2½oz) at start of boil; 28g (approx. 1oz) at 80 minutes

EST. OG: 1053 EST. ABV: 5.2%

TIP 457: *Flavoured porters*

● The recipe for porter makes an excellent carrier for chocolate, coffee and honey, as outlined in Chapters 3 and 4. The easiest way to add chocolate and honey is just to tip the required amount into the copper five minutes before the end of the boil. Adding coffee – a cafetière-full, made as strong as you like and poured into the conditioning tank or bottling bucket – is very easy.

TIP 458: *Barley wine*

● Among the strongest of beers native to Britain, barley wine derives its name not so much from its alcohol content (typically 7–9% ABV, although some are stronger!) as from its vinous quality. A good barley wine can either be as rich, if not as sweet, as an Oloroso Sherry or can have a less-refined, strong liquor-style kick. This recipe will take a week or more to complete its primary fermentation at 18–20°C (64–68°F) and can be left to condition for 3 months before bottling. You may prefer a milder hop than Fuggle.

TOTAL LIQUOR: 37L (9¾ gallons)

Ingredients: 10kg (22lb) pale malt • 400g (14oz) crystal malt • 28g (approx. 1oz) chocolate malt

MASH LIQUOR: 26L (6⅘ gallons)

MASH TIME: 60 minutes

MASH TEMP: 67°C (153°F)

BOIL TIME: 70 minutes

HOPS: 100% Fuggle: 70g (2½oz) at start of boil 28g (approx. 1oz) at 60 minutes; 100g (3½oz) at flame out

EST. OG: 1110 EST. ABV: 11%

TIP 459: Old ale

Old ale isn't so much a distinct beer style as a generic term for any strong ale, whether copper-coloured or dark, that has been well matured. It goes back to the days of 'stock ale', when brewers would produce a very strong beer aged in wood to blend with lighter beers. Among the British brewers, Greene King carries on the practice still, and there remains a handful of other beers that are blends of a strong and a light ale.

TOTAL LIQUOR: 36L (9½ gallons)

Ingredients: 7.2kg (16lb) pale malt • 600g (21⅕oz) crystal malt • 200g (7oz) chocolate malt • 200g brown cane sugar

MASH LIQUOR: 20L (5¼ gallons)

MASH TIME: 90 minutes

MASH TEMP 66°C (151°F)

BOIL TIME: 90 minutes

HOPS: 100% Goldings: 75g (2⅔oz) at start of boil; 28g (approx. 1oz) at 80 minutes

EST. OG: 1080 EST. ABV: 8.5%

LAGER

Note that all the beers in this section require a Czech or German Pilsner yeast strain.

TIP 460: *Pilsner*

⚫ The pale lagers of Pilsen in the Czech Republic were first brewed in 1842 and were a by-product of the same technological breakthrough that had already allowed the brewers of Burton-on-Trent to produce pale ales in Staffordshire – the use of coke in malting. Pilsen, like Burton, was not far from a major coalfield. The same industrialisation that allowed English pale ales to dominate their home market – steam locomotion – also allowed pale Pilsner lagers to be sold throughout German-influenced central Europe, including Switzerland, Poland, the countries of the Austro-Hungarian empire, the Balkans, northern Italy, the Scandinavian countries, the Netherlands and the easternmost parts of Belgium and France.

TOTAL LIQUOR: 31L (8$^1/_5$ gallons)

Ingredients: 4.5kg (10lb) Pilsner malt

MASH LIQUOR: 13.5L (3$^1/_2$ gallons)

MASH TIME: 60 minutes

MASH TEMP: 63°C (145°F)

BOIL: 60 minutes

HOPS: 100% Saaz: 46g (1$^3/_5$oz) start of boil; 20g ($^3/_4$oz) at 50 minutes; 20g at flame out

EST. OG: 1050 EST. ABV: 4.5%

TIP 461: Helles

⊛ Lager brewers in other industrialised regions of central Europe also wanted to brew pale-gold variants of the dark lagers they already produced, and naturally enough they wanted to identify their versions with the original. This wasn't too popular with the brewers of Pilsen itself, for obvious reasons. After much to-ing and fro-ing between the various courts in the dozens of jurisdictions involved, many brewers settled on calling their products simply 'Hell' or 'Helles' – 'pale'. This did not originally denote a style, merely a legal compromise, but today 'Hell' or 'Helles' is generally taken to mean a less-refined everyday lager.

TOTAL LIQUOR: 32L (8½ gallons)

Ingredients: 4.25kg (9⅓lb) Pilsner malt • 280g (9⅘oz) carapils • 280g Vienna malt

MASH LIQUOR: 16.5L (4½ gallons)

MASH TIME: 60 minutes

MASH TEMP: 62°C (144°F)

BOIL: 60 minutes

HOPS: 100% Spalt: 50g (1¾oz) at start of boil; 25g (⅘oz) at 50 minutes; 18g (⅔oz) at flame out

EST. OG: 1055 EST. ABV: 5.5%

TIP 462: Dunkeles

● Not all of the industrial brewers of the mid-19th century German-speaking world had easy access to coke, and in many areas darker lagers made of malt kilned over charcoal remained the norm for generations. Munich, being surrounded by distinctly unpetrified forests, remained the capital of dunkel, or dark lagers, well into the 20th century.

TOTAL LIQUOR: 32L (8½ gallons)

Ingredients: 2.5kg (5½lb) Lager malt • 2.5kg Munich malt • 100g (3½oz) chocolate malt • 100g carapils

MASH LIQUOR: 15.5L (4 gallons)

MASH TIME: 60 minutes

MASH TEMP: 65°C (149°F)

BOIL: 60 minutes

HOPS: 100% Mittelfrüh: 28g (approx. 1oz) start of boil; 20g (¾oz) at 55 minutes

EST. OG: 1055 EST. ABV: 5.5%

TIP 463: Vienna lager

⬤ Vienna found itself in the same situation as Munich, and for decades continued to produce darker lagers. They have almost died out there now, and the two best-known brands of Vienna lager, Negro Modelo and Dos Equis, are Mexican. This has nothing to do with the 3-year reign of Emperor Maximilian, who, although Austrian, was imposed upon Mexico, briefly supported, then scandalously abandoned, by the French emperor Napoleon III. It has more to do with the German diaspora of the mid- to late 19th century, when (speaking very generally) Protestant German emigrants headed for North America and Catholic German emigrants, including Austrians and Bavarians, headed for Latin America.

TOTAL LIQUOR: 32L (8½ gallons)

Ingredients: 4.25kg (9⅓lb) Vienna malt • 750g (26½oz) Munich malt • 28g (approx. 1oz) chocolate malt

MASH LIQUOR: 15.5L (4 gallons)

MASH TIME: 60 minutes

MASH TEMP: 65°C (149°F)

BOIL: 60 minutes

HOPS: 100% Hersbrucker: 30g (approx. 1oz) at start of boil; 28g (approx. 1oz) at flame out

EST. OG: 1055 EST. ABV: 5.5%

TIP 464: *Schwarzbier*

⬤ Much blacker and more 'roasted' than Dunkeles, Schwarzbier remained popular in Poland, East Germany, Estonia and Czechoslovakia during (and after) the Iron Curtain years. Malt grists are more reminiscent of British dark ales than German ones, and may be a hangover from the lively trade British brewers enjoyed with the Baltic in the 18th century. Some Schwarzbiers have even identified themselves as stouts and porters, although they are in fact true lagers.

TOTAL LIQUOR: 32L (8½ gallons)

Ingredients: 3.5kg (7¾lb) Pilsner malt • 700g (24⅔oz) Munich malt • 250g (8⅘oz) Melanoidin malt • 250g CaraMunich malt • 112g (4oz) black malt

MASH LIQUOR: 14.5L (3⅘ gallons)

MASH TIME: 75 minutes

MASH TEMP: 62°C (144°F)

BOIL: 60 minutes

HOPS: 100% Hersbrucker: 32g (approx. 1oz) start of boil; 56g (2oz) at 60 minutes; 40g (1⅖oz) at flame out

EST. OG: 1045 EST. ABV: 4.5%

TIP 465: *Bock*

🔘 In the Middle Ages Einbeck in Lower Saxony became a renowned brewing town and an exporter of strong, dark, top-fermenting and – crucially – hopped beers. Much of this found its way to Bavaria, and the Bavarians rather adopted the style, although adapting it to their own brewing conditions meant it became a style of bottom-fermented lager.

TOTAL LIQUOR: 35L (9¼ gallons)

Ingredients: 3kg (6⅔lb) pale ale malt • 2kg (4⅖lb) Munich malt • 1kg (2⅕lb) Pilsner malt • 500g (17⅔oz) carapils

MASH LIQUOR: 19.5L (5⅕ gallons)

MASH TIME: 75 minutes

MASH TEMP: 65°C (149°F)

BOIL: 60 minutes

HOPS: 28g (approx. 1oz) Perle at start of boil; 14g (½oz) Hallertau at 30 minutes

EST. OG: 1065 EST. ABV: 6.5%

TIP 466: Doppelbock

● This is a stronger version of Bock that was originally brewed by the Munich monks, supposedly to provide sustenance during periods of fasting such as Lent and Advent. Known as 'Salvator' beer, it became 'Doppelbock' when it was sold outside the monasteries to the public. It doesn't contain double the amount of ingredients of a 'single' Bock, as many people think, but certainly packs a punch and warms the soul.

TOTAL LIQUOR: 32L (8½ gallons)

Ingredients: 4kg (8⅘lb) Pilsner malt • 3kg (6⅔lb) Munich malt • 500g (17⅔oz) CaraMunich malt

MASH LIQUOR: 15.5L (4 gallons)

MASH TIME: 60 minutes

MASH TEMP: 65°C (149°F)

BOIL: 75 minutes

HOPS: 28g (approx. 1oz) Perle at start of boil; 28g Hallertau at flame out

EST. OG: 1075 EST. ABV: 7.2%

TIP 467: *Maibock*

⚫ A light amber beer brewed for the spring months. It retains much of the malt flavour of the darker versions, and has quite a high ABV, but offers perhaps less body and texture.

TOTAL LIQUOR: 35L (9¼ gallons)

Ingredients: 6kg (13¼lb) Pilsner malt • 3kg (6⅔lb) Munich malt

MASH LIQUOR: 15.5L (4 gallons)

MASH TIME: 75 minutes

MASH TEMP: 65°C (149°F)

BOIL: 75 minutes

HOPS: 28g (approx. 1oz) Perle and 28g Northern Brewer at start of boil

EST. OG: 1073 EST. ABV: 7%

TIP 468: *Eisbock*

⚫ A strong, dark beer reputedly created as a result of an accident, whereby an innkeeper left his regular Bock outside in the snow by mistake. The beer partly froze in the cask, thus concentrating the alcohol and also conferring a distinct smoothness. Although freeze distillation requires a licence, here's a recipe that will at least recreate the strength.

TOTAL LIQUOR: 40L (10½ gallons)

Ingredients: 6kg (13¼lb) Pilsner malt • 5kg (11lb) Munich malt • 500g (17⅔oz) CaraMunich malt • 500g chocolate malt

MASH LIQUOR: 15.5L (4 gallons)

MASH TIME: 75 minutes

MASH TEMP: 65°C (149°F)

BOIL: 75 minutes

HOPS: 35g (1¼oz) Perle and 35g Northern Brewer at start of boil

EST. OG: 1075 EST. ABV: 7.2%

GERMAN SPECIALTY BEERS

TIP 469: *Märzenbier*

⊕ High summer in Bavaria can be uncomfortably hot, and well into modern times brewing was a chancy business. The custom, therefore, was to brew one last big batch in March, make it strong and hoppy, and start tapping it in July. By the time brewing could begin again after the new grain and hop harvests, the last of the Märzenbier would be truly delectable.

TOTAL LIQUOR: 33L (11²⁄₃ gallons)

Ingredients: 4kg (8⁴⁄₅lb) Vienna malt • 800g (28¹⁄₅oz) Munich malt • 850g (30oz) carapils

MASH LIQUOR: 12L (3¹⁄₅ gallons)

MASH TIME: 65 minutes

MASH TEMP: 65°C (149°F)

BOIL: 75 minutes

HOPS: Perle 28g (approx. 1oz) start of boil; Hallertau 7g (¹⁄₄oz) at 45 minutes

YEAST STRAIN: Oktoberfest

EST. OG: 1057 EST. ABV: 5.3%

TIP 470: *Kölsch*

A beer peculiar to the city of Cologne (Köln), it has to be brewed within the city limits to use the name. Originating in the 13th century, the beer is the city's rebuff to lagers and Pilsners. A light, golden top-fermented ale, it has a slender body, subtle fruit and malt notes on the nose and a dry, slightly sharp palate. It is matured like a lager for 1–2 months and served in very distinctive cylindrical glasses, the production and style of which is governed by law!

TOTAL LIQUOR: 32L (8½ gallons)

Ingredients: 4kg (8⅘lb) Pilsner malt • 500g (17⅔oz) Munich malt

MASH LIQUOR: 15L (4 gallons)

MASH TIME: 75 minutes

MASH TEMP: 63°C (145°F)

BOIL: 75 minutes

HOPS: 100% Spalt: 40g (1⅖oz) at start of boil; 28g (approx. 1oz) at flame out

YEAST STRAIN: German ale

EST. OG: 1045 EST. ABV: 4.6%

TIP 471: Alt

⊛ Another top-fermented ale, Alt is produced mainly in Düsseldorf and Hanover. The name means 'old' and refers to the style of beers brewed before the arrival of lagers and Pilsners. A deep amber to bronze colour, with a hint of esteriness and a good level of bitterness, are a few of the characteristics of the style. Normal strength is around 5% ABV.

TOTAL LIQUOR: 30L (8 gallons)

Ingredients: 2.5kg (5½lb) Pilsner malt • 2.5kg Munich malt • 250g (8⅘oz) Vienna malt • 250g Melanoidin malt

MASH LIQUOR: 16.5L (4⅓ gallons)

MASH TIME: 75 minutes

MASH TEMP: 65°C (149°F)

BOIL: 75 minutes

HOPS: 100% Spalt: 84g (3oz) at start of boil; 42g (1½oz) at 70 minutes; 42g at flame out

YEAST STRAIN: German ale

EST. OG: 1046 EST. ABV: 4.7%

TIP 472: Dortmunder export

🔘 This is a lager beer style distinctive to the city of Dortmund. Usually dark gold to amber in colour, it has some sweetness on the palate, which gives way to a dryish finish. This beer was a big favourite in the city's steel and coal industries in the late 1800s. Alas, today's brews are but a shadow of their former glory, but one or two good examples remain, such as that brewed by DAB.

TOTAL LIQUOR: 30L (8 gallons)

Ingredients: 4.5kg (10lb) Pilsner malt • 500g (17⅔oz) Munich malt

MASH LIQUOR: 16.5L (4⅓ gallons)

MASH TIME: 60 minutes

MASH TEMP: 62°C (144°F)

BOIL: 60 minutes

HOPS: 100% Tettnang: 40g (1⅖oz) at start of boil; 28g (approx. 1oz) at 55 minutes; 14g (½oz) at flame out

YEAST STRAIN: German Pilsner

EST. OG: 1050 EST. ABV: 4.8%

TIP 473: *Rauchbier*

⬤ This beer divides opinion; you'll either love it or loathe it. Phenolic and smoky, the style is synonymous with the city of Bamberg in Bavaria, where today nine breweries still produce this very distinctive beer. The malt is dried over beechwood fires, which give it distinctive colours and flavours that make for a very complex end product. A good-quality smoked malt is essential when making this beer.

TOTAL LIQUOR: 32L (8$\frac{1}{2}$ gallons)

Ingredients: 3kg (6$\frac{2}{3}$lb) Pilsner malt • 1kg (2$\frac{1}{5}$lb) smoked malt • 1kg Munich malt • 250g (8$\frac{4}{5}$oz) caramalt

MASH LIQUOR: 15L (4 gallons)

MASH TIME: 60 minutes

MASH TEMP: 62°C (144°F)

BOIL: 60 minutes

HOPS: 28g (approx. 1oz) Saaz at start of boil

YEAST STRAIN: Oktoberfest

ESTIMATED OG: 1052 ESTIMATED ABV: 5%

TIP 474: *Roggenbier*

Again from Bavaria, this top-fermenting beer gets its very distinctive taste, which is spicy and nutty with a slightly sour note, from the addition of rye malt. The hop character is low, allowing the grain character to dominate. This recipe may well produce a slight haze because of the wheat malt content, but don't worry. Its colour ranges from light to mid-brown.

TOTAL LIQUOR: 32L (8½ gallons)

Ingredients: 3kg (6⅔lb) Pilsner malt • 1.5kg (3⅓lb) rye malt • 1.5kg wheat malt

MASH LIQUOR: 15L (4 gallons)

MASH TIME: 60 minutes

MASH TEMP: 65°C (149°F)

BOIL: 60 minutes

HOPS: 28g (approx. 1oz) Hallertau at start of boil and 14g (½oz) at 50 minutes; 14g Tettnang at flame out

YEAST STRAIN: German ale

EST. OG: 1050 EST. ABV: 5%

BELGIAN ALES

TIP 475: *Pale ale*

● Pale ale is very easy to drink, with delicate hop and malt notes that belie its strength. It can be enjoyed chilled and is quite refreshing.

TOTAL LIQUOR: 32L (8½ gallons)

Ingredients: 4.5kg (10lb) pale malt • 500g (17⅔oz) caramalt

MASH LIQUOR: 15L (4 gallons)

MASH TIME: 60 minutes

MASH TEMP: 65°C (149°F)

BOIL: 75 minutes

HOPS: 100% Saaz: 40g (1⅖oz) at start of boil; 56g (2oz) at 65 minutes

YEAST: Belgian or Saison strain

EST. OG: 1052 Est. ABV: 5.2%

TIP 476: *Saison*

Originally brewed in summer to slake the thirst of farmworkers as they toiled at haymaking and mowing, it used to be far weaker than today's high ABV versions. It's a very complex beer, light in body, with spice and citrus notes and a lasting finish.

TOTAL LIQUOR: 32L (8½ gallons)

Ingredients: 2.5kg (5½lb) pale malt • 2.5kg Pilsner malt • 500g (17⅔oz) wheat malt

MASH LIQUOR: 15L (4 gallons)

MASH TIME: 60 minutes

MASH TEMP: 65°C (149°F)

BOIL: 75 minutes

HOPS: 28g (approx. 1oz) Styrian Goldings at start of boil; 14g (½oz) Saaz at 50 minutes

YEAST: Saison strain

EST. OG: 1055 EST. ABV: 5.7%

TIP 477: *Strong golden ale*

⚫ Epitomised by the Duvel brand, this style of beer is, like the dubbels and trippels, one to be savoured as the ABV is usually around 8%. It should be hoppy and slightly citrusy on the nose, while the flavours can be dominated by spice. The beer is quite effervescent, with a big head and high carbonation in the mouth. It can be served either chilled or at room temperature.

TOTAL LIQUOR: 32L (8½ gallons)

Ingredients: 5.5kg (12lb) Pilsner malt • 500g (17⅔oz) carapils • 750g (26½oz) Belgian candi sugar (white)

MASH LIQUOR: 15L (4 gallons)

MASH TIME: 75 minutes

MASH TEMP: 65°C (149°F)

BOIL: 75 minutes

HOPS: 28g (approx. 1oz) Golding at start of boil; 14g (½oz) Styrian Golding at 55 minutes; 14g Styrian Golding at flame out

YEAST: Belgian ale strain

EST. OG: 1075 EST. ABV: 7.8%

TIP 478: Abbey beer

⚫ Monks exiled to Belgium during the French Revolution started brewing both to provide for their communities and to sell for an income. Two centuries on, the descendants of these brews are generally strong, rich beers, either pale or brown in colour. Most of them, it must be said, are no longer brewed by monks! The handful that still are classify as Trappist beers, but in the vast majority of cases the ecclesiastical trappings are not much more than branding.

TOTAL LIQUOR: 32L (8½ gallons)

Ingredients: 4.5kg (5lb) Pilsner malt • 250g (8⁴⁄₅oz) caramalt • 250g Munich

MASH LIQUOR: 15L (4 gallons)

MASH TIME: 60 minutes

MASH TEMP: 65°C (149°F)

BOIL: 75 minutes

HOPS: 100% Styrian Golding: 28g (approx. 1oz) at start of boil and 50 minutes

YEAST: Belgian ale strain

EST. OG: 1065 EST. ABV: 6.5%

TIP 479: Abbey dubbel

Usually a darker and slightly sweetish style compared to other Abbey beers. The colour can be deep brown or dark garnet, and the beer has a delicate nose and palate, exhibiting notes of chocolate, caramel and vine fruits. The ABV ranges between 6.5 and 7%, but they are deceptively drinkable! Good-quality Belgian candi sugar (dark) is essential for this recipe.

TOTAL LIQUOR: 32L (8½ gallons)

Ingredients: 5kg (11lb) Pilsner malt • 500g (17⅔oz) caramalt • 500g Belgian candi sugar (dark)

MASH LIQUOR: 15L (4 gallons)

MASH TIME: 75 minutes

MASH TEMP: 65°C (149°F)

BOIL: 75 minutes

HOPS: 100% Styrian Golding: 28g (approx. 1oz) at start of boil and 55 minutes

YEAST: Belgian ale strain

EST. OG: 1068 EST. ABV: 7%

TIP 480: *Abbey trippel*

A much lighter-coloured beer than dubbel, it is golden or almost orange in some instances. Although not as rich in character, it nonetheless has a complex flavour that can be both spicy and fruity with a dry finish. The strength ranges between 7 and 9% ABV. Switch to lighter coloured candi sugar for this beer.

TOTAL LIQUOR: 32L (8½ gallons)

Ingredients: 6kg (13¼lb) Pilsner malt • 500g (17⅔oz) caramalt • 1kg (2⅕lb) Belgian candi sugar (white)

MASH LIQUOR: 20L (5¼ gallons)

MASH TIME: 75 minutes

MASH TEMP: 65°C (149°F)

BOIL: 75 minutes

HOPS: 100% Styrian Golding: 32g (approx. 1oz) at start of boil and 55 minutes

YEAST: Belgian ale strain

EST. OG: 1085 EST. ABV: 8.75%

TIP 481: *Lambic beer*

More and more home brewers are experimenting with this style of beer now that specific yeast strains (brettanomyces and *Lactobacillus delbrueckii*) have been produced for sale to help recreate the fermentation process and the myriad of flavours that result from it. Belgian brewers traditionally let their hops age for up to 3 years before using them, to reduce the flavour and alpha acid content. Raw wheat adds both sharpness and spiciness. The beer needs to be left to ferment for 6–8 weeks.

TOTAL LIQUOR: 32L (8½ gallons)

Ingredients: 4kg (8⁴/₅lb) pale malt • 250g (8⁴/₅oz) flaked wheat or wheat malt • 250g raw crushed wheat (if available; if not double up on flaked or malted wheat)

MASH LIQUOR: 18L (4¾ gallons)

MASH TIME: 90 minutes

MASH TEMP: 65°C (149°F)

BOIL: 75 minutes

HOPS: 28g (approx. 1oz) Styrian Golding at start of boil

YEAST: Lambic blend

EST. OG: 1050 EST. ABV: 5.5%

WHEAT BEERS

TIP 482: *Weizen*

◉ Weizen almost died out in Bavaria in the 1970s, when it was considered old-fashioned and rather working class, but it suddenly gained popularity among students (perhaps because it was cheap), sales picked up, the breweries' interest in the style was rekindled, and before long it was on sale all over the world. A pale, hazy, golden brew, its big foamy head is usually shown off by the use of very tall glasses. Very phenolic on the nose, with whiffs of banana and clove, it can be a little off-putting to some. However, the flavour is complex and very refreshing. Bitterness is light and the strength is usually around 5% ABV.

TOTAL LIQUOR: 32L (8½ gallons)

Ingredients: 2.5kg (5½lb) Pilsner malt • 2.5kg wheat malt

MASH LIQUOR: 15L (4 gallons)

MASH TIME: 60 minutes

MASH TEMP: 62°C (144°F)

BOIL: 75 minutes

HOPS: 28g (approx. 1oz) Hersbrucker and 14g (½oz) Saaz at start of boil

YEAST: Weizen strain

EST. OG: 1048 EST. ABV: 4.7%

TIP 483: Berliner/Bremer weisse

● This is a sharp, tart style of wheat beer that was once known as the 'Champagne of the North'. The high acidity, derived from lactic acid bacteria, is similar to that of a Lambic fermentation. The beer is very light-bodied and dry, with a much lower ABV than Bavarian wheat beers, and displays very subtle hints of lemon and fruit on the nose. Serve chilled as an aperitif or, on a hot day, with a dash of sweet fruit syrup such as raspberry to take the edge off. Adapt the Weizen recipe (left), using only 2kg each of the malts and switching the yeast to a Lambic blend.

TIP 484: Weizenbock

● This is a darker, richer, and rather stronger version of Bavarian wheat beer that is brewed in Munich.

TOTAL LIQUOR: 32L (8½ gallons)

Ingredients: 1kg (2⅕lb) Pilsner malt • 2kg (4⅖lb) wheat malt • 3kg (6⅔lb) Munich malt • 112g (4oz) chocolate malt

MASH LIQUOR: 18L (4¾ gallons)

MASH TIME: 60 minutes

MASH TEMP: 62°C (144°F)

BOIL: 75 minutes

HOPS: 50g (1¾oz) Saaz at start of boil

YEAST: Bavarian wheat strain

EST. OG: 1062 EST. ABV: 6.1%

TIP 485: *Witbier*

Belgian white beers, like their German counterparts, almost died out before becoming hugely popular around the world in the 1980s, when revivalist Peter Celis started exporting his Hoegaarden brand. The style displays more fruit and spice on the nose than its German cousin due to the inclusion of Curaçao orange peel and crushed coriander seeds in the recipe. It's a great partner to Indian- and Asian-style cuisine. It can be served well chilled as the flavours are strong enough to carry through. Good-quality orange peel and lightly crushed fresh coriander seed help bring out the best in this brew.

TOTAL LIQUOR: 32L (8½ gallons)

Ingredients: 2.5kg (5½lb) pale malt • 2.5kg wheat malt

MASH LIQUOR: 15L (4 gallons)

MASH TIME: 60 minutes

MASH TEMP: 62°C (144°F)

BOIL: 60 minutes

HOPS: 32g (approx. 1oz) Saaz at start of boil; 28g (approx. 1oz) each of dried Curaçao orange peel and crushed coriander seed at 55 minutes

YEAST: Belgian Witbier strain

EST. OG: 1048 EST. ABV: 4.8%

TIP 486: *Kriek and Frambozen*

● These two major fruit-flavoured Lambic brews traditionally feature either the very small and sour Schaarbeek cherries or wild raspberries, both of which give a very distinctive edge to the beer. A surprising quantity of fruit is required – 1kg (2⅕lb) of cherries or raspberries to every 3–4L (6⅓–8½ pints) of beer in the FV is not unusual. Shop-bought cherries and raspberries will produce beers that are not quite as sharp as the Belgian originals. The length of time in the FV is key to getting as much out of the fruit as possible. Make up the Lambic recipe shown earlier, add 3kg (6⅔lb) of pulped cherries or raspberries to the FV, and allow it to ferment out over 2–3 weeks. The ABV will rise due to the sugar content in the fruit.

TIP 487: *Raspberry wheat*

● This is a fruit-flavoured wheat beer as opposed to the sharper, drier Frambozen above. It's a great beer to enjoy over the summer months. Use the basic Belgian Witbier recipe (see Tip 485) but omit the Curaçao peel and coriander seeds and instead add 2kg (4⅖lb) of raspberry pulp to the FV. Use a regular Belgian ale yeast strain. Again, the ABV will rise due to the fruit sugar content in the pulp.

TIP 488: *American wheat*

⬤ The American wheat style is actually quite different from its Belgian and German cousins, with far fewer phenolics on the nose and more citrus/spicy notes due to the late addition of hugely aromatic US hop varieties. You can substitute the hops in this recipe for Australian or New Zealand aromatic varieties such as Galaxy and Motueka.

TOTAL LIQUOR: 32L (8¹/₂ gallons)

Ingredients: 2.5kg (5¹/₂lb) pale malt • 2.5kg wheat malt

MASH LIQUOR: 15L (4 gallons)

MASH TIME: 60 minutes

MASH TEMP: 62°C (144°F)

BOIL: 60 minutes

HOPS: 20g (³/₄oz) Citra at start of boil; 28g (approx. 1oz) Cascade at flame out

YEAST: American wheat beer strain

EST. OG: 1048 EST. ABV: 4.8%

SEASONAL AND SPECIAL ALES

TIP 489: *Nettle beer*

The idea is to balance the earthiness of the nettle with a very citrusy hop in a very light beer. This recipe uses 100g (3½oz) of nettle leaves at the start of the boil; for a more delicate flavour, try adding 500g (17⅔oz) at flame out instead.

TOTAL LIQUOR: 31L (8⅕ gallons)

Ingredients: 3kg (6⅔lb) pale malt • 1kg (2⅕lb) lager malt

MASH LIQUOR: 10L (2⅔ gallons)

MASH TIME: 60 minutes

MASH TEMP: 65°C (149°F)

BOIL TIME: 60 minutes

HOPS/FLAVOURING: 36g (1¼ oz) Fuggle, 100g (3½oz) fresh-picked nettle tips at start of boil; 20g (¾oz) Citra at 50 minutes; 20g Styrian Goldings at flame out

YEAST: English ale strain

EST. OG: 1040 EST. ABV: 4%

TIP 490: *Elderflower beer*

 This recipe attempts to showcase the elderflower's distinctive flavour by brewing what is almost a light mild with very little alcohol and hop character to mask it.

TOTAL LIQUOR: 34L (9 gallons)

Ingredients: 3kg (6⅔lb) pale malt • 250g (8⅘oz) white sugar

MASH LIQUOR: 8L (2 gallons)

MASH TIME: 90 minutes

MASH TEMP: 67°C (153°F)

HOPS: 28g (approx. 1oz) Whitbread Golding at start of boil; 500g (17⅔oz) elderflower florets at flame out

YEAST: English ale strain

EST. OG: 1030 EST. ABV: 3.2%

TIP 491: *Pumpkin ale*

● Pumpkins are synonymous with autumn. To give this beer a fullness and roundness appropriate to the season, and to complement the spices, it's brewed with a hefty dose of Munich malt.

TOTAL LIQUOR: 32L (8½ gallons)

Ingredients: 3.5kg (7¾lb) pale malt • 1kg (2⅕lb) Munich malt • 500g (17⅔oz) wheat malt • 1.5–2kg (3⅓–4⅖lb) lightly roasted cubed pumpkin

MASH LIQUOR: 12L (3⅕ gallons)

MASH TIME: 60 minutes

MASH TEMP: 65°C (149°F)

BOIL TIME: 70 minutes

HOPS/FLAVOURINGS: 14g (½oz) Magnum at start of boil; 10g (⅓oz) Hallertau Mittelfrüh, 1 stick cinnamon, 2 cloves, 1tsp crushed fresh ginger at 65 minutes

YEAST: American ale yeast

EST. OG 1050 EST. ABV 5.2%

TIP 492: *A light base for stone fruit beers*

● Plum porter is a popular modern beer, although peaches and apricots probably show themselves better in something a little less robust (this is, of course, entirely a matter of personal taste). A traditional American cream ale is pretty much the perfect carrier: add 3.5kg (7¾lb) of chopped fresh fruit (without the stones!) to the conditioning tank or use ready-made puree instead, remembering to check the label to see how concentrated it is and adjusting the quantity accordingly. An alternative carrier would be a Belgian-style Witbier, but without the Curaçao orange peel and coriander seeds.

TOTAL LIQUOR: 33L (8¾ gallons)

Ingredients: 5kg (11lb) pale malt • 500g (17²⁄₃oz) flaked maize

MASH LIQUOR: 14L (3¾ gallons)

MASH TIME: 60 minutes

MASH TEMP: 65°C (149°F)

BOIL TIME: 70 minutes

HOPS: 22g (¾oz) Centennial at start of boil; 32g (approx. 1oz) Mount Hood at flame out

YEAST: American ale strain

EST. OG: 1055 EST. ABV: 5.5%

TIP 493: *Winter warmer*

⬤ Traditionally, in the northern hemisphere, many brewers added a winter warmer to their range from December to March, which was often no more than a slightly stronger version of their house special bitter, or alternatively a weaker version of their house barley wine. This version is perhaps closer to the former, although the late addition of honey will noticeably enrich it.

TOTAL LIQUOR: 33L (8¾ gallons)

Ingredients: 5kg (11lb) pale malt • 250g (8⅘oz) crystal malt
• 100g (3½oz) chocolate malt •100g torrefied wheat

MASH LIQUOR: 14L (3⅔ gallons)

MASH TIME 60 minutes

MASH TEMP: 65°C (149°F)

BOIL TIME: 75 minutes

HOPS/FLAVOURINGS: 28g (approx. 1oz) East Kent Golding at start of boil; 10g (⅓oz) Progress at 60 minutes; 500g (17⅔oz) honey at 70 minutes; 10g Target at flame out

YEAST: English ale strain

EST. OG: 1062 EST. ABV: 6.2%

TIP 494: *Christmas cracker*

● Here's an opportunity to put that tincture of Christmas spices (see Tip 168, page 93) to use in a barley wine to warm the cockles. And if cinnamon and ginger and all the rest aren't to your taste, you don't have to use the tincture; even without them, you'll still end up with a potent and delicious sipping beer. Alternatively, you could try an addition of 500g (17²/₃oz) of honey 5 minutes before flame out.

TOTAL LIQUOR: 36L (9¹/₂ gallons)

Ingredients: 7kg (15²/₅lb) pale malt • 400g (14oz) crystal malt • 800g (28¹/₅oz) carapils

MASH LIQUOR: 21L (5¹/₂ gallons)

MASH TIME: 60 minutes

MASH TEMP: 67°C (153°F)

BOIL TIME: 90 minutes

HOPS: 100% Fuggle: 56g (2oz) at start of boil; 28g (approx. 1oz) at flame out

YEAST: Champagne strain

EST. OG: 1090 EST. ABV: 9.5%

HISTORIC BEERS

The following recipes are taken from *Old British Beers & How To Make Them*, with kind permission from the Durden Park Beer Club, which has been researching and replicating historic beers for almost 50 years.

TIP 495: *Gruit ale (1080og)*

⚫ Until the 1400s, gruit was used alongside hops to flavour and preserve ale. The precise recipe is unknown, but it's thought that the main ingredient was *Myrica gale,* a bitter, astringent shrub that is used today as a natural insect repellent. Many other herbs can be used, including marsh rosemary, yarrow, laurel, alecost, mugwort, horehound, ground ivy, and heather. Here is a recipe for a strong version; but you are of course free to tweak it. The herbs are used dried but not crumbled, and are added in a mesh bag.

TOTAL LIQUOR: 32L (8½ gallons)

Ingredients: 4.5kg (10lb) pale malt • 3.5kg (7¾lb) crystal malt

MASH LIQUOR: 15L (4 gallons)

MASH TIME: 210 minutes

MASH TEMP: 66°C (151°F)/77°C (171°F)

GRUIT: 7.5g (¼oz) sweet gale leaves; 7.5g marsh rosemary (*Ledum palestre*); 7.5g yarrow (*Achillea millefolium*)

BOIL TIME: 20 minutes

YEAST: ale type

EST. OG: 1080 EST. ABV: 7.5%

Make a stiff mash at 66°C. Maintain at 66°C for 3 hours, then increase to 77°C for 30 minutes. Sparge at 85°C (185°F) to achieve the required volume. Boil with the herbs for 20 minutes. Strain and cool. Ferment with an ale yeast. Condition, preferably in wood, for 3–4 months.

TIP 496: *Welsh spiced honey ale* (1070og)

⬤ As early as Anglo-Saxon times the Welsh were famous for brewing with honey, often called 'braggot' or 'bracket' from the Old Welsh *bragaud*, meaning 'honey'. Whether you consider braggot to be an ale or a mead depends on the proportion of malt to honey the beer has. This version, from the early 15th century, is definitely an ale. Keep your refractometer handy in the later stages of fermentation; the beer is not intended to attenuate all that well in order to leave plenty of residual sugars.

TOTAL LIQUOR: 32L (8½ gallons)

Ingredients: 7kg (15⅖lb) pale malt • 500g (17⅔oz) light DME • 1.5L (3⅕ pints) honey

MASH LIQUOR: 15L (4 gallons)

MASH TIME: 210 minutes

MASH TEMP: 66°C (151°F)/77°C (171°F)

SPICES: 60g (2oz) crumbled cinnamon; 60g bruised white peppercorns; 30g (approx. 1oz) diced fresh ginger; 15g (½oz) whole cloves

YEAST: ale yeast

EST. OG: 1070 EST. ABV: 6%

Mash the pale malt as above and ferment with an ale yeast. Dissolve the honey and DME in a little hot water and add to the secondary fermentation along with the spices in a mesh bag. Ferment down to a gravity of 1020, strain, prime and bottle. Allow to mature for 6 months.

TIP 497: Tudor table beer

🏵 Hops were just beginning to infiltrate everyday domestic brewing when this recipe was in use in the mid-16th century. The charge may be small, but it's all added at the beginning of the boil for maximum extraction.

TOTAL LIQUOR: 32L (8½ gallons)

Ingredients: 3.75kg (8¼lb) pale malt • 1.75kg (3⅘lb) amber malt • 400g (14oz) wheatmeal • 400g oatmeal

MASH LIQUOR: 15L (4 gallons)

MASH TIME: 210 minutes

MASH TEMP: 66°C (151°F)/77°C (171°F)

HOPS: 35g (1¼oz) Fuggle or Golding at start of boil

BOIL TIME: 60 minutes

YEAST: ale yeast

EST. OG: 1055 EST. ABV: 5%

Boil the wheat and oats for 10 minutes and add to the mash. Mash as above; boil with all the hops for 90 minutes. Ferment as normal.

TIP 498: Old ale

⚫ The high alcohol content and heavy hop rate mean this late Georgian old ale (dating from about 1820) will need a long maturation period. The very old-fashioned 'double mashing' method is rather complicated, too. But your patience will be rewarded!

TOTAL LIQUOR: 36L (9½ gallons)

Ingredients: 9kg (19⅘lb) pale malt

MASH LIQUOR: 22L (5⅘ gallons)

MASH TIME: 90 minutes

MASH TEMP: 65°C (149°F)

BOIL: 90 minutes

HOPS: Goldings: 300g (10⅗oz) at start of boil; 150g (5½oz)10 minutes before flame out

YEAST: English ale (double pitch)

EST. OG: 1085 EST. ABV: 8%

Make a stiff mash of 2.5L (5 pints) of liquor per 1kg (2⅕lb) of malt. Mash for 90 minutes. Start sparging slowly, collecting the first runnings in a bucket and testing the gravity frequently with a refractometer until the gravity drops to 1070. Then stop both the sparge and collection. Set these first runnings aside and cover with a lid. Restart the sparge and collect a second lot of runnings directly into the copper until the gravity falls to 1035, then stop. Boil the second runnings, thereby concentrating the wort, until the gravity climbs back to 1070. Now add the first wort collection to the copper containing the reduced second wort and boil for 90 minutes with the bittering portion of the hops; this should bring the gravity up to 1085. Rouse often. Condition, preferably in oak, for a year.

TIP 499: Scottish stock ale

Like the old ale, this beer (which dates from 1896) calls for double mashing and long maturation. Unlike the old ale, though, it wasn't really intended to be drunk on its own. Like the 5X still made by the English brewer Greene King, it was a blend that could either be liquored down to a required strength and bottled or casked, or could be used in more complicated blends. Once you've brewed it, however, it's up to you what you do with it!

TOTAL LIQUOR: 36L (9½ gallons)

Ingredients: 5kg (11lb) pale malt • 2.5kg (5½lb) carapils

MASH LIQUOR: 22L (5⅘ gallons)

MASH TIME: 90 minutes

MASH TEMP: 65°C (149°F)

BOIL: 90 minutes

HOPS: 280g (9⅘oz) Goldings at start of boil

YEAST: English ale

EST. OG: 1098 EST. ABV: 9.5%

TIP 500: *Ebulum*

● To round off this book, a digestif that would round off the most splendid banquet imaginable: a rich, strong, port-like unhopped ale flavoured with elderberries. It requires very long maturation – at least 6 months – to allow the elderberries' high tannin content to mellow. Use the double mashing method described above.

TOTAL LIQUOR: 30L (8 gallons)

Ingredients: 10kg (22lb) pale malt • 3.5kg (7¾lb) elderberries, lightly toasted and bruised

MASH LIQUOR: 18L (4¾ gallons)

MASH TIME: 90 minutes

MASH TEMP: 65°C (149°F)

BOIL TIME: 20 minutes

YEAST: English ale strain

EST. OG: 1100 EST. ABV: 10%

INDEX

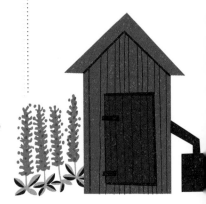